The Salts of the Earth

G000155513

The Salts of the Earth

Eve Crawford

The Pentland Press Limited
Edinburgh • Cambridge • Durham • USA

First published in 2000 by
The Pentland Press Ltd.
1 Hutton Close
South Church
Bishop Auckland
Durham

British Library Cataloguing in Publication Data.
A Catalogue record for this book is available
from the British Library.

ISBN 1 85821 758 X

Typeset by CBS, Martlesham Heath, Ipswich, Suffolk

Printed and bound by Antony Rowe Ltd., Chippenham

DEDICATION

To all those folk who have enriched my life along the way
and woven a colourful tapestry.

CONTENTS

ILLUSTRATIONS

FOREWORD

In *The Salts of the Earth* Eve Crawford has written gratefully and impressively of the people who contributed to her colourful and interesting life. Throughout her narrative she demonstrates her respect for those who perhaps, in other circles, would be classified as 'ordinary'. One of the discernible merits of *The Salts of the Earth* is the clear authenticity which the author exhibits in her portrayal of people whom she met at various stages of her life, a life mainly spent in rural Essex and, strange to relate, in distant Zambia. The Salts are not well-known, prominent citizens in church. social or political life: they are 'ordinary' people whose lives have contributed in a deeply significant way to the life of Eve.

Eve has known and valued the personalities of her acquaintances who have influenced her and who have never been allowed to fall into oblivion. They have remained with the writer throughout her life, her memory and gratitude never failing. And Sam, the cat, must not be forgotten. Eve writes, 'I hope, however, that Sam and I can enjoy each other's company for a little while longer in this imperfect world as we journey together.' Friendship remains the key to all those manifold relationships.

Eve's grandparents, Jeremiah and Ann Maria Clarke, lived in Chevington, a small, scattered village south-west of Bury St Edmunds where my father and I first saw the light of day. Jeremiah Clarke was a farm labourer on one of the farms owned by the Reverend John White, the Squire of the parish, who owned an impressive Georgian house known as The Grove, three farms and over twenty cottages. Jeremiah was a very faithful employee, who complied with all the rector's many requests. When his children – and there were eleven of them – exhibited an interest in the village Primitive Methodist Church, built in Chevington in 1799, Jeremiah was assiduously circumspect to instruct his family to keep their heads low when walking past the laurel hedge in front of the large, impressive eighteenth-century rectory so that the rector, his wife and staff would not be able to discern an employee's family advancing towards the nonconformist stronghold.

The Reverend John White, the third White to hold the living in succession, sold his estate to the neighbouring Marquis of Bristol, the Lord of the Manor, in 1898.

Joseph Clarke, one of Jeremiah's younger sons, who would have attended the village school for a short time, later married Emily Outten from Essex. The school was the same school that my father and his eleven brothers and sisters attended and where I, many years later, was a pupil up to eleven years of age. On their marriage Joseph and Emily, Eve's parents, settled in Essex where they had met. In her childhood Eve was occasionally taken to visit her grandparents in the old thatched cottage and other relations in the village, including her uncle Ted, the youngest son in Jeremiah's family.

Early references in *The Salts of the Earth* to my home village and Eve's conversations with me have undoubtedly deepened my fascination with Eve's memories of her Uncle Ted, her father's brother, whom I knew well as a boy. He, like his father Jeremiah, was a farm worker who, in his spare time in the evenings, acted as an occasional village barber. On two or three occasions I was instructed by my mother to walk down to Farrow's Meadow to the thatched cottage and ask Mr Clarke if he would kindly cut my hair for which she had given me the grand sum of sixpence. I well remember Ted, an ardent supporter, cheering the village football team and offering his instruction to the players. Quietly spoken, Ted was always polite and friendly, courageously tolerating his serious wound of the First World War.

But that is not all. Eve's aunt, Milly Clarke, who was born in the thatched cottage, married an accomplished Chevington Church bell-ringer, Arthur Rolfe, who was a friend of my bell-ringing father. Milly and Arthur's children, Muriel, Dorothy, Vera and Edna, who were Eve's cousins, were contemporaries of mine at Chevington School seventy years ago.

I have discovered all those family connections since reading *The Salts of the Earth* and during the nostalgic conversations with Eve. They have prompted a searching interest in her book, particularly in the Salts themselves, their integrity and the simplicity of their personalities.

The strength of *The Salts of the Earth* certainly lies in the characters of the Salts and I enthusiastically commend it to all who wish to remember life's unsophisticated, but enduring, qualities.

Frank Cooper

Frank Cooper was born in Chevington, Suffolk, where his father was born and where his paternal grandparents had lived since the 1850s and his maternal grandparents since 1902. After attending the village school to the age of eleven, he became a pupil of the West Suffolk County School in Bury St Edmunds, after which he proceeded to Goldsmiths College, University of London and, later, to the Institute of Education of that university. During the Second World War he served in anti-aircraft artillery in Britain and in India.

He taught in Norwich and Colchester, specialising in History, and he served as Headmaster in Keighley, West Yorkshire, and in Chelmsford, Essex. He keeps in touch with Chevington and his writings include *Chevington: a Social Chronicle of a Suffolk Village* and *A Guide and History of All Saints Church, Chevington.*

For many years he served as a trustee of the Chelmsford Educational Foundation and, since his retirement, has been Chairman of the Essex Branch of the Historical Association.

CHAPTER I

MRS MARTIN

Mrs Martin was a lady. I became aware of her soon after I went to work in the offices of a business firm in the town where I lived. I think it was, above all else, her innate dignity which first aroused my interest and awareness of her.

She must have been nearing seventy years of age when I first met her. I had gone early to the office in order to catch up on some arrears of work and arrived before the factory gates had opened. There stood Mrs Martin, looking oddly out of place among the crowd of workers, and almost Victorian in appearance, dressed as she was with utter disregard for current fashion, but neat and trim withal in her black coat and skirt, with a little old-fashioned black hat perched daintily on her coiled white hair, giving her an air of serene dignity. Tiny she was and bird-like in her movements, with an old-world courtesy which was as refreshing as a spring morning.

Mrs Martin cleaned our offices and had been doing so for many years before I appeared on the scene. This work was undertaken with the same care and efficiency and conscientiousness which she would no doubt have applied to the work of the Chairman of the Board had fortune and circumstance decreed that this position should have fallen to her lot. No skimping of time or 'sweeping under the mat' for Mrs Martin. On most days she was there long after the time for which she was paid, making sure that all was in order. Indeed, this, it seems, was partly the cause of her undoing.

Mrs Martin had arthritis and walking was difficult, but I never heard her complain. One of her duties was to carry the sacks of waste paper down a flight of stairs to the yard. I often wondered

1

how the men could run past her down the stairs – intent on their 'important' tasks – and never think of giving her a hand. But she did not think this strange – it was her job and she would seek no favours. When, on occasion, I came across her dragging the heavy sack and took it from her, she would be surprised that I should think she needed help, but accept graciously and with a happy smile.

One morning Mrs Martin was missing and a message from her daughter told us she was in bed with a chill, which eventually developed into bronchitis. Things were difficult for her at home, for she had an invalid husband who relied on her. But when I called to see her, her indomitable spirit was prevailing: she was cheery and optimistic and looking forward to returning to her job. Then for a couple of weeks I was away from the office, and on my return I learned to my consternation that Mrs Martin had been sent her cards and told she was no longer needed as a new cleaner had been appointed in her place. My first feeling was one of incredulity. How could they do this to her? I knew so well what this would mean to her. I was horrified that the 'Management' could sit in their impersonal offices and do this to her. I could not sit back and let it happen.

I knew it was too late to remedy the hurt that I knew Mrs Martin had suffered, but I sought an audience with the Director concerned and he spared me ten minutes from his *important* affairs to talk about Mrs Martin. He was surprised to think that I cared and had chosen to concern myself with the situation. 'But she is old,' he said, and pointed out that, by all the rules, she should in any case be retired; indeed he had kept her on long past the normal age for cleaners. He did not know about the invalid husband and the difficulty they had in making ends meet. Above all he did not know what an all important place this job held in the life of Mrs Martin, giving her, as it did, an interest outside her home – a few hours away from the illness and dependence of her husband, a feeling of belonging and of being of use in the firm for which she had felt an almost maternal concern for so many years, the dignity of knowing her work to be efficiently and conscientiously performed. No, he was being most reasonable – it was obvious that it was time for a younger person to take over. Look how slow she had become –

2

why, she was always there long after the other cleaners had left, and now she had bronchitis and might at any time let us down by not being fit enough to come in. Yes, of course, this was the opportunity to make a change. But she still did her work well, I protested, was still thorough and efficient and was almost better from the bronchitis. Couldn't we just have allowed her to carry on until she herself decided to give up; she most assuredly *would* have given up when she found she could no longer give satisfaction. But no, the action had been taken by this man who was trained to take more important decisions than those concerning the employment of cleaners! My heart was heavy as I left his office.

I went again to see Mrs Martin, feeling ashamed for my 'superiors' – and helpless. Her daughter met me at the door. 'Did you know they don't want my mother back?' she asked. 'This has been a dreadful blow to her; she never thought they would do this to her while she was ill. She hadn't had any time off for sickness for years.' I was shown into Mrs Martin's little sitting room. Her bronchitis was better; in fact the rest and care which her daughter had given her had made her look a little less frail and put some colour into her cheeks. But the light had gone out of her eyes; they looked hurt and defeated, although she still retained her dignity. 'I was so surprised when they sent me my cards,' she said. 'I am better now and was so looking forward to coming back to work. I know my arthritis has made me a bit slow, but I could still manage.' What could I say? I could find no excuse for the hurt that had been done to this gallant lady and I felt my murmured words of comfort and regret to be totally inadequate. 'If there *is* a reckoning day,' I thought, as I left that sad little room, 'I think the action taken by that eminently reasonable Director in his aloof and efficient office is one of the things that will have to be reckoned with, and how surprised he will be to be confronted with it.'

Mrs Martin only lived for a few more years and in even less time she was only a fading memory in the hustle and bustle of the everyday office life. But I shall never forget Mrs Martin or cease to be glad that at least once in my life I was privileged to know a real lady.

CHAPTER II

SUSIE

When Susie came to work in my office I little dreamed of the complications she would bring to my working life. Her elfin features, dainty figure and graceful movements gave the suggestion of a sprite or fairy having fluttered down to live among us. Her gentle mien and soft cadences of voice seemed somehow out of place in the hurly-burly of business life; surely her ethereal personality would have been more suited to the world of arts rather than in a mundane general office where typing and filing were what she was required to do. I never discovered how Susie came to work in an office – whether it was her *chosen* occupation I never knew. In fact there was a lot about Susie which was ever to remain a mystery. You see, among the many intriguing facets of her personality was the existence of the fantasy world in which she moved. Its existence was only very gradually revealed to me and these revelations continued to baffle and intrigue me for as long as our association lasted. Indeed, they were to cause me many a headache and not a few problems as time went on.

Susie's colleagues were fascinated with her stories about her life and the characters who peopled it. It was only gradually that I began to realise that a lot of these facts did not tie up, and she was so convincing and seemingly naive and simplistic that she had us fooled for many months and even years! The problem for me was in telling fact from fiction and, in my job as Welfare Officer with responsibility for the staff, I was confronted with many a dilemma. What an inventive brain little Susie had! Even in some particular incident when she knew that I had managed to sort out the truth she would, with her charmingly deceptive air, still try to cover up with some story equally far from the truth.

On one occasion Susie arrived very late at the office and I was appalled and concerned at her appearance. In place of the normally neat and dainty Susie was a pathetic little figure, dishevelled and distraught. Her clothes were dirty and torn and she showed me various cuts and bruises. After calming her down and attending to her injuries I began to unravel her story. Jimmy, her boyfriend, had been driving the car and they were involved in an accident. They had both been taken to hospital and then she said, quite calmly, 'I think Jimmy is dead.' On questioning her further she said she had seen him taken away on a trolley, unconscious, and she feared he was dead. There were so many unanswered questions, but first I must telephone the hospital and make enquiries about Jimmy. I obtained his surname and learned to which hospital they had been taken. But my enquiries were unfruitful – Jimmy had never been admitted or heard of. Susie, of course, was quick to defend her story and said she was not sure of the name of the hospital, it could have been a different one after all. My exhaustive enquiries still brought no result – there was no Jimmy! Had Susie invented him altogether? My questioning of Susie brought me no nearer the truth as her story got more convoluted and puzzling. Clearly something untoward had happened to her, but what? Had she perhaps been attacked or abused at home maybe? I would never know; gradually she recovered and we got back to normal, leaving just one of the mysteries surrounding Susie for ever unsolved.

We gathered from her conversation that the most important person in Susie's life was her Gran. Gran really spoiled and indulged her. She featured large in all Susie's day-to-day conversation. If she appeared in a new dress, it was Gran who had bought it for her. Bits of jewellery too, were Gran's gifts and she would agree, with a sweet smile, that she was a lucky girl to have such a kind and indulgent grandparent. It seemed that Gran was far more important to her than her own parents, of whom we heard very little, and she spent more time in her Gran's house than in her own. 'Oh, I stayed the week-end with Gran,' or 'I spent the night at Gran's,' we were often told. We really felt we knew Gran.

There was also a succession of boyfriends, whether real or in her imagination we never knew. We heard a lot about them – their names, their looks, their characteristics, where they spent their time, etc. We also heard the reasons they were replaced by their successors! One day we were told that the current boyfriend, Dennis, had decided to change his name and now wished to be called Colin. We thought this odd, but then so were lots of things that Susie told us!

The weeks passed and Colin remained on Susie's horizon; he had lasted longer than his predecessors. Then one day Susie appeared wearing an engagement ring – Colin had asked her to marry him! Knowing Susie, we wondered – was Colin real or was he another figment of her imagination? The ring was real – so we waited as we were regaled with descriptions of Colin and his attributes. We were told he was handsome and resembled Adam Faith. Then wedding plans were discussed and eventually we learned its date, time and venue.

I and two other of my colleagues decided we would go and see Susie married. At least we would know whether it really did happen! Surely she could not con us over something so important! – although I felt that nothing would surprise me. We arrived at the Registry Office – yes, there was a wedding imminent; people were gathered outside and we tried to identify folk from Susie's descriptions – if, indeed, it was her wedding! Then we gathered from conversations overheard that it was indeed Susie who was to be married. We waited – Susie was late. The guests – her family – were getting anxious; did they perhaps sense Susie's unpredictability? However, the bridegroom (Colin?) was assuring people that it would be all right, he was sure Susie would soon arrive. And sure enough, after some delay, she did, looking very young and vulnerable in her simple little white dress. Yes, it really happened – Colin was real and Susie was married!

Well, I have said I thought nothing could surprise me, but I was wrong. What followed not only surprised me but was mightily embarrassing to boot! Susie had previously told us that Gran was not well and it was doubtful whether she would be able to attend the wedding and, of course, we had all commiserated with her, thinking what a great disappointment this would be. After the ceremony, as we were waiting around to see the photographs taken, a mature, plumpish lady approached us. Ah, I thought delightedly, Gran has after all recovered and made it to the wedding. Going forward I greeted her. 'Oh,' I said, 'it's nice to meet you, you must be Susie's Gran,' whereupon the said lady fixed me with a stony stare and said coldly, 'Gran? – no, I'm her mother!' My colleagues looked on in disbelief and horror as I made my confused apologies, wishing I were anywhere but at Susie's wedding! We concluded that after all Gran had really been too ill to attend. As the photographers got busy we were speaking to a young woman who was apparently a friend of Susie's, and then came my second shock. After we had agreed what a charming picture Colin and Susie made, I remarked that it must have been a great disappointment for Susie that her Gran could not be there. The girl looked at me in surprise and puzzlement. 'I don't understand,' she said, 'Susie hasn't got a Gran.' So we encountered the greatest surprise of all – Gran simply did not exist! We were stunned into silence and disbelief. How could we for so long and so completely have been taken in by our devious little Susie?!

The wedding day had certainly been a revelation of the lengths to which Susie's imagination could go, and how completely she had taken us in over such a long period. She had endeared herself to us in many ways and we were genuinely fond of her. The reason for what went on in her mind remained a mystery. Was her homelife so unsatisfactory that she had to invent something quite different, was it just her need for attention, or was it some quirk in her character that caused her to live in her dream world?

Some years later I saw Susie again. This time she was boarding a bus with two young children in tow. She looked the same little Susie, sweet and fragile, accepting with a sweet smile the help with pushchair, etc. readily given by her fellow passengers. But, I wondered had Susie changed? Had her romanticising ceased with the reality and responsibilities of married life? Had Colin perhaps given her the stability and fulfilment in her life so that it was no longer necessary to live in cloud-cuckoo-land and invent life as she wished it to be?

As I think of Susie now, many years later, I still wonder about these unanswered questions and the enigma which was Susie.

CHAPTER III

NOAH

Noah is a black African, a Zambian, and I had the privilege of knowing him when I worked at a training centre in Zambia where he was employed. He was tall and slim and lithe and good to look upon. A serious person was Noah, intense and ambitious, and the flashes of wit and humour which came occasionally were all the more delightful and surprising. I first met Noah when I taught on an adult literacy scheme at the centre and on which Noah was an enthusiastic pupil. He was from the Northern Province and belonged to a different tribe from most of the other pupils; his background, too, had been somewhat different from those brought up in the copper mining area where we were situated. He had lived on the shores of Lake Tanganyika where fishing had been the main industry. This experience rather set him apart in the eyes of his fellow students; most of them, living inland and with no travel facilities, had never even seen a lake or river, let alone having any conception of seas or oceans.

All the pupils, without exception, were keen to learn, having recently gained their independence as a nation, and knowing that an education was of vital importance if they were to play any part in shaping their future. But Noah seemed to have that extra determination to make the most of the opportunities offered to him.

Education was a commodity which had been sadly lacking in the lives of the majority of Zambians. Schools were few and far between and if they did not happen to live within reach of one they were just unlucky unless they went to live with relatives in a different area or were prepared to walk many miles each day, which, of course, many

11

of them did. Even so, as a rule it was only a Primary school education which was available – Secondary schools were even more scarce. If one was available it was not often economically viable for them to attend. No free education for them! – and it was necessary for them to work as soon as they could be useful. When, therefore, the Centre made free English classes available, the African employees' excitement and enthusiasm knew no bounds.

The reason for the instigation of these classes was that the men's limited knowledge of English was causing problems, not only for them, but for the European staff as well. Instructions were apt to be misinterpreted, causing confusion and misunderstanding. For instance, on one occasion two men came to the office with a problem concerning the boiler. The Business Manager, being engaged on the telephone, told them to take a chair and wait until he was free. However, on concluding his conversation the men had disappeared and on reaching the boiler room he found two office chairs ensconced there. 'Well,' they said, 'you told us to take chair.'!

As you can imagine, these English classes were a challenge, both to me and to the pupils alike – but what a happy and interesting time it was for us all. Their determination and enthusiasm and will to succeed more than compensated for the difficulties we all had to overcome. Noah always liked to sit near the front of the class, intent on missing nothing of what was going on, his serious and intense look contrasting oddly with the cheerful, beaming faces around him. For Noah, learning was a serious business! These men had never before possessed a book and their pride and joy in these novel possessions (oh, what a lot we take for granted!) as they carefully brought them out from their wrappings each day – they must not get soiled – I found quite humbling. So it was surprising when one day Noah appeared in class minus his exercise book. When I asked the reason, Noah, looking very confused, launched into a rambling explanation which appeared to make no sense at all. 'Oh, Noah,' I said, 'You've told me this strange story by way of explanation and I don't think much of it is even true!' No more was said and the class continued as we struggled with grammar and vocabulary. Among other words defined that day was the word 'fable'. The next day when I arrived in class Noah was in his usual seat with his exercise book open in front of him. Then he stood up and, looking very serious, said he wished to speak. His speech was by way of a confession and an apology. 'I am sorry,' he said. 'You say we must always speak truth and yesterday I tell you a fable – it was not true; my book, I forgot it!' He sat down looking much relieved: I accepted his apology and the class continued.

The Zambians are a happy people. They live for the moment and that moment is theirs to enjoy. Who shall say their philosophy has not a lot to recommend it? although those who advocate the wisdom of providing for rainy days might have reservations. In my experience complications often arose because, not only did they want to be happy themselves, but they were determined everyone around them should be happy as well. Noah could not bear the thought of making me unhappy by thinking badly of him for forgetting his book, hence his convoluted story. I had been suggesting to them that it was simpler to tell the truth in such circumstances, but this was not easy for them to accept. However, Noah, in his serious and thoughtful way, had decided in this instance that I was right and had, in front of the whole class, made his confession. How important it is that we understand cultures and thought processes other than our own.

Noah was a member of the cleaning staff and his main job was cleaning all the windows on the campus. One day when I came across him at work I remarked on his 'never-ending' job. This remark puzzled him and when I suggested that when he had finished cleaning the vast amounts of glass around the campus it was time to start all over again, he seemed much amused and, thereafter, it was a standing joke between us. I often saw Noah in the course of his work. His enquiring mind was ever alert and sometimes he would present me with a list of words for which he urgently required to know the meaning. The Centre benefited from a large and beautiful library. This had been given by the Swedish people in memory of Dag Hammarskjöld, the United Nations General Secretary who was killed when his plane crashed in the area, and this library I encouraged the men to make use of. This world of books opened new vistas for Noah and presented him with a whole new source of knowledge, especially of other countries and their history, giving him knowledge of things he had never dreamed of. It was also a source of great frustration to him. His eagerness for knowledge was hampered by his limited English vocabulary, making it necessary for him constantly to refer to a dictionary to find the meaning of the words he read – hence the lists which he presented to me! When I discovered he was attempting to read of the American struggle for independence and suggested he might tackle something simpler he said, 'Oh no, I want to learn about these Americans, they were like us, struggling for independence.' Another time his list included the words 'blood, sweat and tears'. 'Noah,' I said, 'You've been reading about Winston Churchill,' and so he had. Oh yes, learning for Noah was a serious business, a great struggle, but also a source of wonder and delight.

At the end of my term, when I was preparing to leave Zambia, there was great consternation among the pupils lest their English classes should come to an end. In the busy life of the Centre a replacement teacher was not easy to find. I, too, was fearful that these men whom I had grown to love and admire would be unable to continue their studies. I think, for a time at least, a replacement teacher was found. Some of them I learned were using their limited cash resources to continue their learning at evening classes. On my return to England I was able to correspond with several of them and

Noah with the author

was delighted to receive news of their progress from time to time. One man, to his joy and delight, had been given work at the Centre as a receptionist – progress indeed. Then I heard that Noah had been appointed nightwatchman. I thought this was progress for Noah, but sadly it proved to be his undoing. One night a burglary took place and apparently Noah was suspected of being a collaborator and, when I heard, had been committed to prison. This was indeed sad news. I wrote, sending a message to Noah, telling him of my concern and after a time he wrote to me. I was not to worry – nothing was wrong – everything was fine. I would never know the truth, but I understood: he, of course, could not bear me to be unhappy and so I must be assured that all was well. I could only hope that it turned out to be so for him.

I often think of my pupils and especially of Noah , of his intellect, his hopes and ambitions and his struggles to get educated against such great odds. I am glad I was privileged to know Noah – maybe he taught me more than I was ever able to teach him.

CHAPTER IV

BILL

I feel sad as I write of Bill – a real country lad he was, solid and reliable. For most of his life he had done an honest job of work on the land and was never overly ambitious. He loved the country life and felt at one with its sights and sounds. The open fields and woods and blue skies were his natural habitat and under the stars at night he felt safe with all the familiar pattern of things he had known all his life. After a hard day's work around the farm and around the fields he was content to return to his little cottage and enjoy the good country fare which his wife Annie had lovingly prepared for him. What could be more delightful on a winter's evening than sitting contentedly by his cosy fireside with his pipe and his thoughts, or maybe talking over the affairs of the village with his equally contented wife.

But the years passed by and brought unwelcome changes, as advancing years are apt to do. His work in the fields and around the farm was taken over by younger and fitter men. Due to advancing years he could no longer walk for hours around his familiar haunts. More and more his little cottage became a safe haven and when, after a short illness, his wife and companion of many years died, he spent more and more of his time in and around that little cottage which held so many memories. There, in his familiar surroundings, he felt safe and secure. With a bit of help in the house he could manage and enjoyed pottering around and taking a pride in his little garden.

Yes, it was lonely at times, but his little home felt friendly; his wife's presence was still there and he often talked to her and felt she understood his moods. So much reminded him of his Annie and of their many years together. He remembered how they had bought the furniture together when they first wed. It was certainly not grand; they could only afford enough for their basic needs, but he remembered, as he looked around him, with what pride and joy they had gathered enough bits and pieces to make a cosy little home. There were also the little additions that, as the years went by, they had managed to accumulate – a picture, a mantel ornament, a pretty vase his Annie had spotted in a shop window on one of their infrequent outings and he had bought for her birthday. Each piece brought some special memory and how precious these memories now were.

Even as, with the advancing years, Bill became more frail, yet he was contented. He and Annie had not been blessed with children, so he had no family to care for him. Neighbours were helpful but they thought it was not good for Bill to remain alone in his little cottage. It was obvious that simple household tasks were getting too much for him and his beloved garden impossible to cope with. With his failing memory, was it safe for him to be alone? And so the practical and helpful Social Services department became involved. Oh yes, they were sensible and reasonable and the arguments they put to Bill for the reasons why he should change his lifestyle could not be faulted. But how could they understand? Bill knew that nobody could ever understand what it would mean to him to live anywhere but in the cottage that had been home to him for so many years and held a lifetime of memories. He was horrified and dismayed at the mere thought and made his feelings known in no uncertain terms! Yes, Bill was stubborn, awkward and unreasonable – terms which quite a few well-meaning people thought applicable!

But at length, Bill, with a sense of the inevitable and with an oh so heavy heart, was persuaded that a bright new room in a sheltered accommodation complex where he would have company and be able to enjoy the care provided, would solve all his problems and allow him to spend the rest of his days in peace and security. Friends and neighbours and Social Services workers were all so good and helpful and did their best to make the transition easy. He was even allowed to take a few of his precious possessions, which was some comfort. The room chosen for him was pleasant; there was even a view of the countryside from his window and this helped too. People told him how fortunate he was, pointing out all the advantages of his new life – the freedom from worry about household arrangements, good meals provided, a bell to press should he need help or feel poorly. Yes, Bill knew all this and he knew that all these people had his best interests at heart, but it was hard to be cheerful and show any interest in his surroundings. Some even said he was ungrateful and was not deserving of all their efforts. But how could they understand? He knew that nobody could ever share his thoughts and know his heartache as he tried unsuccessfully to feel 'at home' in his new environment. The days dragged; all Bill's interest in life had gone, and before many months had passed he slipped quietly away to join his Annie, as he had been longing to do.

Yes, I feel sad as I write of Bill, but how many are in the same circumstances to-day? The advancing years bring many problems. When the years have caught up with us will we too be thought ungrateful and unreasonable and obstinate or will we be able to accept the inevitable with good grace? It's a thought, but only time will tell!

CHAPTER V

MONTY

I write of Miss Montague Graham-Harrison, a lady of the English aristocracy. The misfortune of being christened with a male forename – and 'Montague' withal – befell her because her parents, having been thwarted of producing a male child, would not at least be denied the prerogative of endowing the unfortunate infant with the male name of their choice. However, to her friends – and they were many – 'Monty' was the name by which she was known or as 'Mama Monty' by the Africans among whom she worked and who loved her dearly.

When I first met Monty she had been living for many years in Zambia, where she had gone in her youth to work as a missionary under the auspices of the Anglican Church. In her 'retirement' she had been allocated living accommodation on the campus of the Ecumenical Training Centre where I had gone to work. But 'retirement' was not in Monty's scheme of things – that she would never do and the extent of her involvement in any sphere where she could be of use was truly amazing. Her usefulness in this situation was unparalleled, for none understood the African character better, or could better unravel the nuances of the tribal languages, the misapprehension of which could at times cause problems. Our staff, besides being inter-denominational was also international and, although English was the accepted language of the Centre, language problems could arise, especially with the African staff, so it was to Monty we went when in difficulties.

Monty had lived with the Africans so long that she really identified with them; she had become part of their lives and they of hers. And

21

yet withal she had retained her upper-class English accent, which seemed to contrast strangely with her African way of life and mode of dress! Fashions had long since passed Monty by and, indeed, all material comforts and gracious living were unimportant compared to her work with her beloved African people. This attitude was taken to such lengths that it tended to cause embarrassment to her fellow-workers. Her living quarters were strictly for eating and sleeping; ease and comfort were certainly not her top priorities – even cleanliness often took a back seat as far as her domestic arrangements were concerned. Although we all loved and respected her, invitations to visit Monty for a meal, for instance, could be somewhat of a trial. Other considerations were far more important to her than order and tidiness in her domestic affairs and her mind, being in many places at once, was not always on the matters in hand, resulting, maybe, in a burnt offering or an inadequately prepared one, according to her current preoccupation. That one had to remove evidences of her busyness before one could occupy the chairs seemed to go unnoticed and often she had given scant attention to the cleanliness of the plates from which we ate. So it was with some trepidation that one embarked on a social call, never quite knowing what was in store.

Monty loved animals as well as people and owned a little dachshund that accompanied her everywhere and fitted happily into her way of life. Cats also would never be turned away. On one occasion, one of her cats being in the family way and the birth imminent, she became concerned over its disappearance, but very relieved when she eventually found it ensconced under her bed, happily purring away, having found an exceedingly satisfactory place for her brood among the conglomeration of odd garments and papers which also resided there!

Among Monty's activities, which included running Guide and Brownie packs, was her work giving occupational therapy at the local hospital. My flatmate, who helped her in this enterprise, recounted some hair-raising experiences and often returned home utterly exhausted, frustrated and exasperated having been trying to cope with Monty's erratic methods of operation. She could be irascible and impatient in her eagerness to accomplish her aims, making her not always the easiest of colleagues. The journeys alone were a hazardous ordeal, as her driving was typical of her life-style and just as erratic. She had previously met with a serious accident on the road resulting in head injuries causing damage to her sight and hearing and also to her vocal chords. Typically this had not deterred her from resuming her active life-style. Explaining to me once her inability to participate in any singing, she said, 'I expect the good Lord thought, "We'll put a stop to that – it was never anything to boast about so will be no great loss."' Such a philosophical soul, Monty!

Various pictures of Monty remain in my mind. There was the time that I went with her to see some tribal dancing in a large stadium in the adjacent town. On leaving we walked past groups of Africans sitting around outside, who greeted her enthusiastically with cries of 'Mama Monty!' Hurrying past one group after another, she muttered, 'I don't know who they all are – I expect I taught their grandmothers!'

Then there was the happy occasion when the President of Zambia came to visit us, he being very interested and appreciative of our work among his people. On his arrival the staff were all presented to the President and Monty, having a great sense of occasion, had made a special sartorial effort. She was very well-known and respected throughout the country because of her years of devoted service to the Zambian people and it was not the first time that the President had come into contact with her. I shall always remember them standing chatting together, Monty arrayed in an assortment of garments reminiscent of past days, giving her a slightly Victorian appearance, and the President, his entourage keeping respectfully in the background, thoroughly enjoying their exchange of ideas and reminiscences.

Where I got to know Monty best and to appreciate her wonderful mind was in a Bible Study group held on the campus. There her depth of thought and Christian insight were a revelation and enhanced the respect and affection I shall always feel for this truly great lady.

CHAPTER VI

ESSIE

I met Essie in Zambia where we worked at a training centre for Africans. When I arrived to join the staff it happened that Essie was away on leave, so I first knew of her only by repute. However, even before I met her I felt I already knew this much loved member of staff, who seemed to have impressed her vibrant personality on the whole campus. And when I did meet her eventually, this I could understand.

Essie on campus with her students

Essie had been a missionary sent to Africa by her church in Canada and then directed to Mindolo, the Ecumenical Foundation on the Copper Belt in Zambia where we met. Here she was doing a splendid job as the Director of the Women's Training Centre. This Centre provided training for African women; the courses in Christian Home-Making, varying in length, included classes in sewing, knitting, budgeting, child-care, hygiene, etc. English classes, too, were necessary: the women came from varying backgrounds and in some cases they had no knowledge of English whatever. Secondary schools were, at that time, few and far between, so the general standard of education was low. If education was available it was the male members of the family who were given preference. A choir was formed on each course and very popular it was – the African member of staff responsible for this always managed to get marvellous results. Each woman was allowed to bring one child; families had many children and it was always the youngest who joined us, so, of course, a crèche was necessary where the babies could be cared for while the mothers were in class.

As you can imagine the Centre was a very busy place, full of activity and with never a dull moment. For most of the women, coming away – sometimes long distances and for the first time – from their home environment, was quite traumatic and presented, for them and the staff, quite a few problems. Of course, the person ultimately responsible for sorting out these difficulties was Essie. But for Essie problems were there to be solved and inevitably solve them she did, with amazing cheerfulness and efficiency.

Essie's husband had died early in their marriage and I once asked her if that was what motivated her to change the direction of her life. 'Oh, no,' she said simply, 'God told me that this was what I had to do.' Essie had gone on a retreat and one day, sitting alone on a hillside, God had spoken so plainly that she could not ignore His voice. Oh, yes, she had tried: she was happy in her church and in her teaching career and told God that this thing He was asking of her was ridiculous and not at all in her scheme of things. But He would not be denied and, after much soul searching she knew what she had to do. And, of course, if this was where God had sent her, then He and she together could overcome any difficulties that might come her way.

For a time I worked closely with Essie at the Women's Centre, dividing my time between teaching and working in the office. During that time Essie never ceased to amaze me. Her cheerful, bubbly personality and persistent optimism could make the problems, when they arose, appear not to be problems at all, and even to make one ashamed to have even entertained the thought that they were insurmountable. Just prior to the rainy season, when the atmosphere became very dry, I was prone to lose my voice. I should have realised, when this happened one morning and I told Essie in a hoarse whisper that I could not take my English class, that the word 'can't' was just not in her vocabulary. On her way to more pressing matters she surprised me by casually throwing over her shoulder, 'Oh, you'll manage.' So I had no option, but went, with some trepidation and no voice, to confront my class of thirty women – and manage I did, with signs and gestures and the help of the blackboard! And afterwards, did Essie enquire how I had coped? Of course not, that episode was all in the past; there were all sorts of other things to be concerned with and forward thinking to occupy her thoughts and energies – and, of course, I had managed!

*Essie with some of the women who came on a
Christian home-making course*

27

Owing to the generosity of a charitable organisation a mobile van was purchased. This was fully equipped to teach housewifery skills and intended to be used to teach women in remote village areas. Its arrival had been eagerly awaited and was celebrated in typical African style with joyous and exuberant singing and dancing, with the drums much in evidence. Essie joined excitedly in all the activity, for this was the culmination of a long awaited dream. It was a great day when we all assembled to wish the new venture well, as we watched Essie and her African helper drive off into the bush with this wonderful new equipment. This was a challenge and appealed to her dauntless spirit.

At the end of a course the sheer hard work and responsibility, plus coping with the extreme heat, began to take its toll, although Essie was loth to acknowledge this. However, she had provided for this eventuality by securing a little cabin some miles away in the bush, which provided her with total relaxation. I accompanied her there on one occasion and, just as she threw herself so completely and unreservedly into her work, so she could unwind and give herself up to complete relaxation. What a contrast those days were and how necessary – lovely lazy days with all problems, routines and stresses forgotten, eating when we felt like it, taking a dip in a little nearby pool and sitting lazily beside the river listening to the African wild life – even watching a wily old crocodile taking his daily swim or sunning himself on the opposite bank. What a wonderful way to recharge our batteries and give Essie the renewed vitality and strength to cope with all the stresses which the next course would bring.

On one occasion Essie had gone to the cabin with a friend and one evening as they sat quietly chatting a number of Africans emerged from the bush and gathered outside. They were shouting excitedly and Essie, knowing the local language, knew that they boded no good. It was an ugly situation – two white women surrounded by a crowd of hostile Africans and with no means of summoning help. Marjorie, Essie's companion, was understandably scared and repeatedly asked Essie what it was all about. Although the Africans were using threatening language and Essie knew it was a dangerous situation she remained her cheerful self, trying to allay Marjorie's fears and assuring her that all would be well, at the same time, I am sure, putting up a few prayers that, indeed, it might be so. As it happened, no harm did befall them and the Africans drifted off without carrying out their threats. It was typical of Essie, first of all to shield her friend and then to show such faith and optimism in the face of danger.

In the midst of her busyness it became necessary for Essie to return to Canada for an operation on her foot. We were told it would be some months before she would be fit to return. She kept in constant touch and long before the date given by her doctors, Essie was back on campus, being welcomed with open arms – such was her enthusiasm, and typically Essie.

One day when I was enjoying Essie's company in her home, she was showing me photographs of her early days in Canada. Years in the hot, dry atmosphere of the tropics is not conducive to preserving a youthful appearance and, of course, she had no longer the fresh looks of youth. I remarked on how pretty she looked in the photographs, and Essie replied, 'Yes, what a difference, but then I didn't come out here to grow beautiful, did I?' Yes, Essie had sacrificed even more than her looks: after all, beauty is more than skin deep; Essie is proof of that, and she had certainly got her priorities right.

The President of Zambia was interested in the work of our Centre, as he was in all work that furthered the good of his people, and we had met him several times on his occasional visits. On the occasion of one of these visits Essie happened to be out in the neighbouring town. She was making her way back along the acacia lined driveway when she spied the President's car and following entourage leaving the Centre. On its approach along the driveway she hastily stepped aside to let it pass. However, to her astonishment the whole procession stopped and the President, leaning out of his car, hailed her with a cheery, 'Hallo, Essie, how are you?' and proceeded to ask her about her work and wellbeing. She had evidently made an impression on him on his previous visits and maybe before that in her missionary work in Zambia. But such was Essie's personality that those with whom she came into contact did not forget her – not even Presidents!

Essie is now enjoying a well deserved retirement, but her work goes on and I am sure her influence on the lives she has touched will live on too.

CHAPTER VII

SAM

Sam is now fifteen years old. He has been my constant companion for all of those fifteen years, and now we are growing old together. Yes, for if our year is equivalent to seven of the feline species, then my beautiful Sam is now one hundred and five years old! He does not believe this, for although he perhaps is not so scatty and impulsive as he was in his youth and sleep becomes a more important feature of his daily routine, yet life is good, his days hold many pleasures and his contentment as he indulges in complete relaxation, as only his kind can, is a joy to behold.

Sam came to me at six weeks old from a neighbouring farm where he had been born, the only ginger and white of the litter – just a little golden ball of fluff, his beautiful white front contrasting splendidly with the rest of his thick fluffy golden fur.

It was fun getting to know each other and he was not long in impressing his personality on his little world. And what a handful he proved to be in those early days. His energy knew no bounds and was displayed in ways which sometimes caused me some concern. Everything had to be investigated. Curtains were there to be climbed: scaling furniture was a great challenge as he leapt from one dizzy height to another – maybe he felt the thrill of achievement such as a mere mortal might feel in having scaled Mount Everest or run a marathon! After all these breathtaking escapades he could suddenly relax and the next minute be curled into a fluffy ball, purring with contentment until he drifted off into a pussy's dreamland.

Sam's arrival in my home coincided with a spate of spring

cleaning, and coping with the task of redecorating my sitting room with Sam in attendance proved quite an exciting experience. His exuberant interest in all the activities was quite exhausting (for me, not him!). His movements were like quick-silver and one never knew what his next moves would be. He would suddenly startle me by taking a flying leap from some object of furniture onto the top of the step ladder where I was perched wielding a paint brush, and it seemed his fur was in danger of becoming more white than golden if he came too often in contact with the white paint on my brush! I soon discovered that all furniture surfaces had to be covered, especially the piano top, which came in contact with his sharp little claws.

He has always loved human company and human contact and will show friendliness and affection when shown the slightest encouragement. To me, of course, this was especially evident as he recognised me as his provider and ally. Alternating with his harum-scarum forays around the room he would curl himself around my neck and purr his contentment as he rested there whilst I continued my activities. On one occasion when I was tackling the window paintwork this sight caused some amusement and comment from passers by!

Although cats have no human speech what clever ways they have of communicating – most of it by body language. Sam has a very small voice and uses it rarely, but has a little soft chirrup which he uses as a greeting or to say, 'Here I am, take notice of me.' But to let me know his feelings his body language is most effective. If I have done something of which he does not approve or have failed to grant his wishes he will sit with his back towards me – never facing me – and that eloquent back really does express disapproval. When I return from an absence – maybe a few days holiday – he makes very certain that I am aware that he takes a dim view of my desertion of him. His method then is to ignore me completely – no little chirrups of greeting, no response to my advances, just a turned back and a little face expressing aloofness and disdain. After a time, when he is certain that I have understood, he will decide to offer me his forgiveness. This he will do unstintingly, never in half measures, following me around the house, wanting to be petted and not letting me out of his sight – to make sure, presumably, that I don't sneak out on him again!

He is mischievous and has a sense of humour too, using his wiles to get his own way or to get 'one over' on me in different ways. He has his bed on the back porch and on some summer nights when I call him in he may have other ideas. He chooses not to respond to my calling and on looking up I spy him on the flat roof just above my head and just out of reach. He has a most mischievous expression on his face which seems to say, 'I know you can't reach me; I'm not coming to bed and you know you can't win this one!'

Sometimes he makes a decision which results in a real battle of wills – mostly over food. Oh yes, he has very definite tastes in food,

Sam on the patio

knows exactly what he likes and makes his preferences very plain. He uses his wiles too, to make sure these preferences are deferred to. And this is where our battles of wills come in. In the interests of his health, liver, his favourite meal, cannot be served too often and sometimes has to be alternated with the contents of a tin, which Sam regards as quite inferior. Thus he will get it into his stubborn little head that nothing but liver will do: I am equally determined that his next meal will be the tinned variety – thus an impasse! He will then disdainfully ignore my offering, hoping that I will weaken, until eventually hunger decides the issue. Then, when he is sure I am not observing his defeat, he will, in desperation, clear his dish and walk nonchalantly away to enjoy his siesta with the comfort of a full tummy!

He has an uncanny way of knowing when tasty tit-bits are in the offing. Cheese, I think, he could smell a mile off and will miraculously heave in sight when it is around. He even becomes alert and expectant the minute I get the cheese grater from the drawer before there is even a smell of cheese! Yoghurt is another favourite offering and he again appears from nowhere when it is on the menu and demands his share.

I am always amazed at how much this intelligent wee creature understands of human language. It is said that it is the *tone* of the voice they understand, but I have a strong feeling that their understanding goes beyond even that. Sam, as with most cats I suppose, has his little routines and timing is something he has an uncanny instinct for. How does he know when his normal bedtime comes round? – but he does. He can be comfortably ensconced on my lap, where, at any other time, it would take a lot to make him move voluntarily, and at ten o'clock I say softly, 'Bedtime, Sam,' whereupon he looks up, stretches luxuriously, jumps down and makes tracks for the door.

Although we understand each other and have our ways of communicating, I sometimes would that Sam had the benefit of human speech. I would love to know what thought processes go on in that clever little brain. And is all that intellect and personality made extinct when his time here is over? Who knows? I like to think it will carry on and develop perhaps in another world where all is perfect. I hope, however, that Sam and I can enjoy each other's company for a while longer in this imperfect world as we journey on together.

CHAPTER VIII

WILLIE LONG

His name was Willie Long (the name pronounced 'Willa' in the strong Norfolk accent with which he spoke). He was a Christian and his faith shone through every facet of his personality, making him the unforgettable character that he was.

I was a child when I first met him and the impression he made on my life was strong and lasting. He was then middle aged and came to stay in my parents' home on many occasions during the winter months whilst conducting evangelistic missions at our Methodist chapel in the village. Willie was a Norfolk fisherman and it was only during the winter months, when fishing was not always possible, that he was free to go on his evangelical campaigns which he loved and undertook with a sense of dedication and calling.

He was an attractive personality in every way and not the least of his attraction was his looks. He was a striking figure as he walked around the village dressed in his navy blue fisherman's jersey and wide bottomed navy trousers – tall and well-built, yet exceedingly gentle in manner. His greying hair was silky and curly and I can remember now the lovely feel of it and his gentle chuckle as I sat on his knee and buried my hands in his curls and the softly flowing beard which framed his face. His eyes, like those of so many men of the sea, were blue and penetrating and far-seeing from the habit of scanning the distant horizons. But when one was confronted with all these attractive features, what one noticed above all was the calm radiance that shone from his face, an inner glow that stemmed from the vital and living faith that was in him and motivated his every thought and action. His voice was like a caress and his beautiful singing voice could move a congregation to tears.

Willie Long was born in a Norfolk seafaring family living in the little fishing community of Sheringham. He and his brothers longed for the day when they would be able to take their place with their father in the little fishing fleet which went out for mackerel, herrings, crabs and lobsters. He used to tell us of the proud day when his father first took him on a fishing trip. All eager-eyed, he sat in the boat watching for a sign of a catch; the nets had been spread and all was ready when he noticed the movement of one small fish in the water. Excitedly he called out, 'Here come one, father,' and was rather chagrined at the hearty laughter which followed from the seasoned fishermen, interested as they were in hauling in the fish in their hundreds!

As in the preaching of Jesus, everyday events were woven into His teaching, so in the pulpit Willie would put in many illustrations of his observations and experiences as a fisherman. There was the exciting and dramatic story of a rescue in the Sheringham lifeboat, of which his grandfather, Robert Long, was the first coxswain and in which Willie was one of the crew when his brother lost his life. One really lived the story with him as he recounted this poignant drama in simple yet pertinent language. One could feel the danger as he described the upturning of the boat in the rough and savage seas and share his grief in the tragic loss of a comrade and brother.

Willie – far right – with boat and crew

It was an amazing thing how he could hold an audience enthralled, for his was not in the accepted sense great oratory. His great love for humanity seemed to reach out to everyone and in his simple sincerity lay his greatness as he presented to his congregation the cause of his Lord and Master whom he loved so well.

On one occasion, unknown to Willie, Dr Jarrett, the then famous preacher, was in his audience. I well remember his recounting the incident and can hear his amused chuckle as he expressed his amazement when Dr Jarrett made himself known at the close of the service, the mixture of amusement and awe that he felt as he realised he had actually been preaching to this famous and distinguished man. Such was his humility that he never realised his own greatness.

Willie's visits to our home were always regarded with pleasurable anticipation. He was an ideal guest, considerate and thoughtful and always concerned not to put extra burdens on my mother. This was evidenced in all kinds of thoughtful ways, such as making his own

Willie with Mary

bed and cleaning his shoes. He was always ready, too, to show his appreciation of my mother's cooking, baked apples, I remember, being one of his favourite desserts. To this day the taste of baked apples brings back memories of his happy enjoyment of them.

In his advancing years Willie became blind, but this did not deter him from keeping his preaching appointments. The Scriptures were so well-known to him that written words were unnecessary in the course of his services and the lessons did not need to be 'read', they were there in his memory, and he was able to expound those Scriptures, drawing on the depth of the faith that was part of him and the experience that faith had brought him, and deliver sermons that were vital and meaningful to his hearers. His religion, never a one-sided facet of his life, permeated every part of him, not least his family relationships. He was a wise and loving husband and father, who all his family turned to for understanding and guidance.

One of my last memories of this lovely man is when, in his declining years, my family and I went to visit him at Sheringham. We found him in his favourite spot by the sea, where he was sitting with some of his old fisherman cronies exchanging memories of their time at sea. I can vividly remember how his face lit up as he heard our voices and the exclamation of joy at being together with us again.

I recently went on a pilgrimage to West Runton, where Willie lived towards the end of his life, and visited the Willie Long Memorial Church, built two years after his death and where his memory is very much alive. In the vestibule there were photographs of Willie in his fisherman's garb and, among the tributes, a framed certificate and address presented to him on his having served sixty-five years as a Methodist lay preacher. As I stood there with my memories the church steward came up to greet me. 'Many years ago I knew this man,' I said, 'did you, perhaps know him too?' 'Yes,' he replied, 'I am his grandson.' Willie had always spoken with love and affection of his grandchildren; now I was to meet Robert, a grown man and keeping up the tradition in this little memorial church. How proud and happy Willie would have been. What a joy it was to meet Robert and his wife and to visit them in their home, the home where Willie had spent the last years of his life.

The lady who conducted the service on that Sunday morning told me how Willie had helped and encouraged the group of young people to which she belonged when, as a young girl, she was training to become a lay preacher in the Methodist church. There, in that beautiful little church full of his memories, Willie came alive for me once more. After the service I went with Robert and his wife to visit Willie's grave in the local churchyard. At the foot is appropriately engraved a little sailing boat and on the headstone a verse which he composed shortly before his death. As I stood by his earthly resting place I thanked God for every remembrance of him – a truly humble man but one of the greatest I have ever known.

Willie Long's Tombstone

In cherished memory of William Long
(Willie)
Called home November 1st 1946
Aged 87 years

———————

Now the Lord has brought me
To His glorious home above
To be with Him for ever
In the land of light and love
And for you my dearest loved ones
He makes clear and plain the way
For you to come and join us
In the realm of endless day.

———————

Also
Mary Elizabeth his devoted wife
died June 6th 1949
Reunited

———————

CHAPTER IX

SARAH

I had just come to work in Zambia and knew little of the country and its people. One day Essie, a colleague who had worked as a missionary in Africa for some years, asked me if I would like to go with her to visit Sarah. Eager for new experiences and for the opportunity to meet the African people, I readily agreed to accompany her. On the way Essie talked to me about her friend Sarah. I learned that she was a very old Zambian lady, quite how old nobody knew – not even Sarah herself – for at that time there was no birth registry in existence in the country. She was blind and she lived alone and her home was a little mud hut. Early on she and her family had come under the influence of the English missionaries and had become devout Christians.

As we drew near the compound where Sarah lived she emerged from her little hut, a wizened little body in an odd assortment of clothes, and on her face was a beaming smile of welcome. Although blind, her hearing was acute; she had heard our footsteps approaching and had recognised Essie's voice. Her delight at 'seeing' us was unmistakable. As Essie told her she had brought a friend to visit, Sarah turned to me with a delighted smile lighting up her face and grasped my hands in both her own as she greeted me in her tribal tongue. The Zambians are a very polite people and for them it is always important to greet a visitor with a warm welcome. But this was more than a formal greeting – it was so obviously giving her pleasure that we were there. She talked excitedly to Essie who was conversant with her language and could respond to her exuberant welcome. Then, surprisingly, Sarah began to sing, her face alight with happiness, the words of the hymn probably remembered from her early contact with the missionaries. Her high quavering voice was in perfect pitch as she sang the words, in English, of the children's song, 'Jesus wants me for a Sunbeam to shine for Him each day'. We joined with her as she sang, standing in the African sunshine surrounded by a gaggle of interested little boys and girls! and an assortment of goats and hens and other animals.

Then Sarah led us into her 'home'. To say that it was basic would be an understatement. When my eyes had become accustomed to the dim interior, I discerned on the mud floor a bed of sorts with an assortment of ragged covers and a small wooden chest which I suppose served as a table and also held her meagre possessions. That was all – that was Sarah's home – and she was content!

Essie had once knitted Sarah a woollen sweater for use in the chilly mornings and evenings of June and July. On her next visit, on enquiring if the garment had been useful, Sarah explained philosophically that she hadn't got it any more – the rats had eaten it!

The Africans would never let a member of their extended family lack what they could supply and I am sure Sarah would have been daily provided with food and her basic needs met. For the most part her life would be lived outside in the fresh air and the hut simply used as sleeping accommodation. When I suggested to Essie that the hut might be made more comfortable for her with, perhaps, added furniture, a chair maybe – she said, no, Sarah wanted nothing different; she could find her way around, it was all familiar and she wanted nothing more.

I came away from my visit to Sarah feeling very humble. We westerners in our modern and affluent society demand so much more than Sarah possessed to ensure her happiness and well-being. With all our possessions and with the benefit of modern technology giving us the enhanced lifestyle we have come to accept as the norm, have we achieved that inner happiness and contentment which she so obviously possessed, or are we better people in consequence? – I fear not!

Sarah had sung 'Make me a Sunbeam' – she was already that and a shining example to all of us who may be inclined to moan about our lot. The sunbeam that she prayed to be – and was – has radiated beyond her ken. When I am inclined to become depressed or irritated by minor trivialities I think of Sarah and feel its glow!

CHAPTER X

POPPET

She broke into my life quite suddenly, like a bright ray of sunshine, a little five year old bundle of fun and laughter, mixed with the uncanny sense and wisdom of maturity. Poppet I called her when she came to live with me and she fitted into my life and home as happily and naturally as if we had always been together, although I had hardly known this grandchild of mine until then.

She was in appearance a sturdy little person, with her feet firmly on the ground, but what was most in evidence was her bright beaming smile and the joy of living that shone from her big brown, trustful eyes. Poppet loved her fellow human beings, never seeing their faults and never believing that they would wish her anything but good. Age never seemed to be any barrier to the goodwill and friendliness which she generously offered to all my friends as well as those of her own age group.

The power she had to adapt to her suddenly changed situation amazed me. Getting her settled in at school, another totally new experience and one which I had feared might be traumatic, was a most happy and natural event. From her first introduction to school life she was happy to extend her friendship and trust to teachers and fellow pupils alike and her enthusiasm for all the activities of her broadening world knew no bounds. From that time on our house seemed to be overflowing with the variety of children she would bring home – all introduced as 'my friend'. This love for her fellows could indeed be embarrassing at times when it extended to folk other than children, such as the time in the park when, as was her wont, she engaged a complete stranger in conversation and promptly

47

invited him home to tea! One feared at times lest this trustful innocence should be betrayed. She was indeed a delight to know and among my friends and acquaintances, 'a real little charmer' was how I frequently heard her described.

Beside these delightful childlike qualities Poppet showed a strange maturity beyond her years and her companionship could be almost adult. She was intensely practical; things mechanical fascinated her and when on one occasion I bought a new Hoover, her delight and excitement knew no bounds as she busily fitted it together and couldn't wait to test its efficiency. Any household gadget was a great source of interest to her, as indeed all the household arrangements were, and nothing delighted her more than 'helping' around the house and garden. And she went about these tasks with the common sense and ingenuity of a seasoned adult.

These contrasting facets of Poppet's personality were fascinating and a constant source of interest and surprise, providing me with never a dull moment. Indeed, on occasion this little extrovert's high spirits, sense of mischief and zest for life could be most disconcerting

Poppet aged 9

as it turned upside down my former sober and predictable routines. One amusing incident occurred when I took her and her small brother with me when shopping in a supermarket. I had sat my small grandson of about three years old in the seat of the shopping trolley which I pulled behind me and eventually arrived at the check-out. When I looked round in the course of emptying the trolley I was amazed to see this small boy sitting there quite unconcerned, but plastered from head to foot with sticky price tags, which Poppet had found and decided to relieve her boredom by putting them to this unique use. Yet, on other shopping expeditions she would be a most helpful companion, once, I remember, finding the appropriate department long before I did and saying busily, 'Come Crawfie, here it is, now we must have a *deep* look.'

Her amazing capacity for grasping life with both hands and living life to the full could sometimes be quite exhausting and, indeed, land her in my bad books, such as the times when she would be so busy and absorbed enjoying life with her young companions that she would have complete disregard for the time and come home eventually to spoilt meals and having caused me worry concerning her welfare and whereabouts. But whenever she was punished for some misdemeanour with deprivation of pocket money or by being banished to her room, it was always accepted philosophically and without complaint. Being confined to her room was the worst punishment she could have, as being deprived of the company of her fellow human beings was indeed a sore trial. There might be a few tears but after a while I would hear her singing happily away to herself and she would emerge her old sunny self again, bearing no grudges, the past put firmly behind her and ready to face life again with all her accustomed zest and vigour.

Eventually boarding school beckoned for Poppet and she entered an exciting new world, enjoying all the new activities with her own peer group and coming home for the holidays with her horizons broadened, new friends made and exciting opportunities ahead.

Poppet is grown up now and making a useful and fulfilled life for herself in her chosen career. She is no longer part of my life and I see her seldom, but I shall always be grateful for the happy years we spent together and for the enrichment she brought to those years.

CHAPTER XI

DEREK

Derek is my window cleaner, and a good window cleaner he is too. Not only does he delight in making the glass clear and sparkling, but will not have the job spoiled by leaving dirty window sills, so cleans the paint-work as well! It was a good day for us both when he came to my door offering to clean my windows. I have learned a lot about Derek since and we have become good friends.

Derek was not always a window cleaner and it was the last thing he had ever dreamed of doing. Oh, no, he was a high flyer, was Derek, a keen business man and a finance broker no less. Life was rosy and getting better all the time. He and his wife were the envy of many with their luxurious life style – a beautiful home, large cars and not a care in the world. Good holidays and socialising with their large circle of acquaintances pleasurably filled their leisure hours. What reason would they have for thinking it would ever be any different? Rainy days were not on the horizon so why should they be provided for? Money was there for spending and enjoying all it could provide.

When the blow came the shock was, understandably, devastating. Was it bad luck, mismanagement, the recession, betrayal of colleagues he thought he could trust or maybe a combination of things – whatever the cause, Derek's world fell apart. The possessions that had given him security and stability and cushioned him against life's ills were gone; his houses, his cars and his work too, which had assured his independence and social standing had all been swept from under his feet. So-called friends, too, were conspicuous by their absence and the devastation even proved too

51

much for his wife to cope with and so their marriage fell apart too. Derek was really down to rock bottom! Life as he had known it was no more – what was there to live for? For a time he felt it was not worth the struggle and contemplated what seemed to be the easy way out.

But in the end Derek was made of sterner stuff and something – was it his guardian angel giving him strength? – enabled him to plumb the depths of his inner resources and haul himself up from the Slough of Despond, to believe in himself again and accept the challenge to start afresh. Oh, no, it was not easy, for what had he to start with? Well, he had his health and strength and now, the will to face a challenge. There was no money to train for a new career, nor to provide equipment for a new business venture. But wait – he *could* manage to buy a ladder and a bucket. Hey presto! He was now in business again – as a window cleaner! There was one snag – Derek had no head for heights and climbing ladders needed some courage. However, this was a small obstacle compared with the many he had already overcome. Of course, an area abounding in bungalows was the answer until he had mastered climbing the dizzy heights of upper storeys! It was not all plain sailing and there were frustrating and disappointing times when people didn't want to know when he knocked on their doors offering his services. But his cheery friendliness and the conscientious service he gave soon won him customers until he had obtained enough work to keep the wolf from the door.

Derek's priorities had changed: no longer was the accumulation of wealth and possessions his consuming passion. He had learned that the simple life had many compensations. Gone were the stresses and strains and tensions of the modern business world. He was savouring small pleasures and kindnesses he had not noticed before; he was enjoying his life in the open air and at the end of the day found contentment and satisfaction in a job well done. He found he was making new friends, too, the type of friends he had never had before. They were mostly among his customers in whom he took an interest and was always willing to give them a helping hand. In return he was often invited in for a cup of tea and a friendly chat. Now he is never short of work, for he is often asked to do various other jobs for his customers, including painting and decorating, at which he has become adept. It is good to have a handyman to call on when needed and I, too, have benefited from Derek's helpfulness in using his new-found skills.

Derek came to see me to-day. His smile seemed even brighter than usual and there was a definite sparkle in his eye. He has found another friend, a very special one this time, and is engaged to be married! Things are indeed looking good for Derek my window cleaner, and who is to say he doesn't deserve it! Who was it who said that every cloud has a silver lining and that disasters can sometimes be blessings in disguise!

CHAPTER XII

MIJA

Mija is a Zambian and proud of it. He is motivated by a great loyalty to his country and his race and his purpose in life is to become educated, no sacrifice being too great in the pursuit of this ambition. Mija is also a happy man, as are most Zambians, and this happiness and zest for life is a wonderful thing to behold as it shines out from his strong black countenance.

When I met Mija he was head groundsman on the campus of the Training Centre where I had gone to work. This was a responsible position and of this he was fully aware as he conscientiously carried out his duties, including the supervision of the rest of the ground staff. His living quarters were not on the campus and somewhere in the adjoining township he had another life with his wife and children, but of this I knew nothing.

To wander around the campus grounds was a joy and the beautiful brilliantly coloured African shrubs and flowers really gave of their best under the loving care bestowed upon them by Mija and his colleagues. The vegetables, too, were his pride and joy and his face would glow with pride and happiness as one wandered around and congratulated him on the fine array of produce. The little orange grove was a real picture as well as being full of a delightful aroma in the flowering season, and no less a joy later on when the trees were hung with myriads of golden fruit. Among the shiny, ragged banana trees and tall paw-paws he could be seen moving happily around, and whatever the work of the moment – watering, hoeing, clearing of the ground or the picking of the fruit – Mija's happy industry would be evident.

55

Following Zambia's Independence there was, and still is, a great yearning for knowledge and the Training Centre was being used to capacity, with various courses being run for Africans from many parts of the Continent. Then one happy day the Principal had an idea – why should not the Zambian staff who worked in the kitchens, the dormitories and the grounds have the opportunity to learn too? This decision was made partly because the European staff, coming as they did from many different countries, were speaking the English language in so many varied accents, thus making a very real language problem for the African staff whose English was, for the most part, decidedly limited.

It was agreed that I should start these English classes and when the men learned of this innovation there was great excitement and anticipation among them. Mija's cup of happiness was now overflowing and his eyes were alight with renewed zest for life as he said with a great sigh of wonder and contentment, 'I shall now be a student.'

Some of the men had never had an opportunity to go to school and for them the idea of reading and writing opened a new world of delight. But Mija had been to school and had reached Standard VI, the equivalent of reaching the top of Junior School in England. On the morning of our first lesson he was right there in the front row with his newly acquired books spread out in front of him, his face and manner showing a happy determination to face any challenge that might present itself. And Mija needed this determination, for to him the learning of English was no mean task and needed much concentration and perseverance. And perseverance Mija certainly had, coupled with an insatiable thirst for knowledge from whatever source it was to be obtained.

In the course of our lessons we used for our reading a simple Geography book which someone had given me. Mija was full of questions about the contents of the book and it was then I realised how little the men knew of any country outside their own. I can still recall Mija's wide-eyed wonder and amazement as we read about the different countries of the world and discussed and compared sizes and populations and the ways and customs of different nations.

Luckily Mija had the capacity to laugh at himself; this was a good thing as it helped to offset the seriousness with which he regarded the difficulties he experienced in mastering the English language and coping with the composition of grammatical sentences. Many a laugh we had together as we read through his attempts at English composition and I tried to unravel the complicated jumble of words which he had tried to construct into a sentence, and when at last I would arrive at the obscure meaning of what he was trying to say – 'Yes,' he would say with a delighted laugh and a sigh of relief, 'that is what I was meaning.'

The enthusiasm of the men for these classes was not a 'flash in the pan'. Week by week the men came, just as keen at the end of a year as they had been at the first lesson, determined to gain all they could from this unexpected opportunity that had miraculously been presented to them. And always Mija was there in his place when I arrived, in the middle of the front row, well prepared for the lesson and with the light of battle in his eyes!

Mija and paw-paw tree

57

At the end of that first year I set them an examination. This was a great event for them and was taken most seriously by all the men involved. In the following days I was besieged as I walked around the campus by the men who couldn't contain their impatience and anxiety to know, 'Have I passed?' – 'Did I do well?' Then we staged a 'Graduation' ceremony at which the men demonstrated their reading ability and read essays which they had written during the year. Mija had been chosen to make a speech. This he had prepared very carefully and delivered with great dignity, thanking the Principal for giving them the opportunity to learn and me for being their teacher. Indeed, it was a happy and moving moment for me when he said of me with obvious sincerity, 'She has taught me many things which I did not know.' What a joy it was to share in their sense of achievement.

Now that I am back in Britain I so often think of Mija and others like him, with admiration for their courage and tenacity in the face of odds, and wonder what opportunities they have since had to achieve their ambition to be 'educated'. I often think that if our children here could meet men like Mija, it would be a salutary lesson and surely make them appreciative of their educational opportunities.

CHAPTER XIII

ANNIE

To-day I went to Annie's funeral and as I sat in the parish church, full of folk who in some way Annie's life had touched, there was a strong feeling that Annie was there with us and I felt she was glad we had come to say our last farewells for she always loved to have her friends around her. If Annie had lived for a few more weeks she would have made her century, but no, she would not have been one hundred years *old*, for a person younger in spirit it would have been hard to find.

Annie had been born locally and had never moved far from her birthplace; indeed, in all her life her travels had never taken her outside the county of Essex. In our small town she had a large circle of friends and was much loved and cherished.

I only knew Annie during the last years of her life, but how glad I am that I was given this privilege: one's life could not help but be enriched through contact with her. When I visited her in her tiny cottage we spent many happy times together as she recounted tales of her early life, when with her indomitable spirit and simple faith she had weathered hard and difficult times.

Annie's life style was simple in the extreme and her worldly possessions few. She lacked what most of us would term to be basic necessities – no central heating or double glazing for Annie, no washing machine or even a fridge, not even a bathroom – and the loo was at the bottom of the garden! But a happier, more contented soul than Annie you would never wish to meet. Her valiant spirit would not allow her to be intimidated by circumstances or by events which would have proved overwhelming for lesser mortals. Her faith was almost tangible and gave her the peace and assurance which permeated her life. Yes, she was one with Julian of Norwich in her view that 'all must be well'. To illustrate: when, well into her nineties, one summer night it became necessary for Annie to make the journey down the garden, she fell and, although not badly hurt, was unable to get up. And there, the next morning, a neighbour found her. And yes, Annie was still smiling. 'Don't worry,' she said, 'I'm all right; I've been listening to the birds and watching the stars – it was such a lovely night!'

Annie's father was a farm worker and, in the days when a tied cottage went with the job, the employer held all the cards; a farm hand's life was certainly not his own. Long hours were the accepted norm and whatever conditions were laid down, there was no way they could be questioned. In Annie's father's case it appeared that not only he was subject to the rules applied, but the farmer claimed jurisdiction over the children too, for Annie told me how she and her brothers had to be up at 6 a.m. and work for a couple of hours before school gathering acorns which the farmer fed to his pigs!

Annie was nothing if not resourceful and brought her resourcefulness and common sense to bear, at an early age, in dealing with awkward situations. This she had to do when one day she was sent to the village to buy bread. It was getting dusk and it was a long walk along the lonely country road. After a time she heard in the distance footsteps which seemed gradually to be coming nearer and, on looking fearfully round, she saw that a stranger was following her. This fact alone made her fearful for at that time strangers in the village were a rarity. She instinctively knew that she had to put distance between herself and her unknown follower and hurried on as fast as her little legs would take her, eventually breaking into a run as she neared the baker's shop and arriving thankfully but somewhat out of breath. Apparently, courageously, little Annie did not think of acquainting the shopkeeper with her fears, although she knew that she now had to face the journey home. On leaving the shop with her bread, she looked fearfully around thinking the stranger might be lurking in the shadows. Then, plucking up her courage she started on her homeward journey. At that moment, to her delight, a horse and cart came lumbering slowly along the road and Annie's relief was great as she walked in safety beside it until she arrived home. 'Didn't you ask the driver for a lift?' I asked her as she related her story. 'Oh, no,' said Annie, 'I knew I'd be safe if I just walked alongside.' How typical of her to maintain her independence and cope with the situation without involving anyone else in her problems.

Annie was brought face-to-face with the realities of life and death at an early age. She helped to care for her aged grandmother who lived in the family home and one morning she was sent to tend the fire in her room. She turned on hearing her grandmother call, ran over to her bed and, as Annie so often related, 'Before I could call for help she just died in my arms.' This was a traumatic experience for a young girl, the memory of which remained as a very vivid memory for the rest of her life.

The farthest that Annie ever travelled from her home was to Leigh-on-Sea, some forty miles away, where she took a post as maid in a bank manager's household. This was for her a great adventure and her face always lit up with pleasure as she recounted her experiences there, where she was apparently appreciated for all that she did for the family. Annie loved children and was delighted to find she was to help care for the small daughter of the family. This little girl was a great joy to her and she loved especially their afternoon walks around the seaside town. Everything was new and exciting and the shops a wonder to behold. Annie loved to talk to me about this period of her life as I knew the district well and, although it had all happened to her some eighty years before, she could still remember the walks they had taken together and even the names of the streets they had traversed. She was so surprised and delighted that I, too, knew these streets and could share her experiences of so long ago. I think too, that that little girl was also impressed with Annie and that the love Annie showed her was reciprocated, for she still kept in touch and was concerned for Annie's welfare in those last years of her life.

Yes, Annie loved children although, sadly, she never had any of her own. She married during the first world war and her husband was invalided out of the army while still young. He was then only able to do light work and so life was always a struggle – not that

Annie ever complained. In fact, in all our talks and whatever experience she was relating never once did I hear her complain of her lot – nor in my hearing did she ever speak ill of another person. The circumstances of life were accepted without question whatever their import, the knocks dealt with philosophically and stoically and the good times looked on as a bonus and enjoyed to the full. Yes, a great philosopher was Annie! Her faith was an integral part of her life, essentially simple but so absolute and unshakeable that it had brought her through all the vicissitudes of life with patience, courage and equanimity.

In her extreme old age Annie was often lonely. She loved company and had many friends dropping in during the day for a chat, but also, inevitably, there were many lonely hours, when, as she said, 'I think of all my friends and pray for them all.' Any suggestion of her going into a home to be looked after was vigorously brushed aside. So many years her little cottage had been her home and different surroundings were unthinkable – and so her friends made life as good as it could be for her. One of her chief joys was a telephone which had been installed. Now she could talk to her friends and this she did with regularity and felt less isolated. Her delight and gratitude was like that of a child with a new toy. Annie loved reading, too, and was grateful to be supplied with magazines which I took her from time to time. They were so enjoyed that they were never thrown away, but, in her thoughtfulness, were passed on to friends so that they could enjoy them too. And Annie, in all her life, had never worn glasses – how remarkable, but then Annie was just that!

Then one day I went to call on Annie and was greeted with the sad news that, after a fall in her cottage, she had been taken to hospital and, sadly, that proved to be her last journey. She lived for several weeks and was her usual cheerful self, delighted to see all who visited her, throwing up her hands in a typical gesture of joy at being surprised by a visitor, and typically grateful for all that was done for her. But sadly, she just failed to make her century, when lots of celebrations had been planned for her – maybe there were even better surprises awaiting her in her heavenly home when, one day, she slipped peacefully away from us.

Yes, I like to think Annie was with us to-day as we said our farewells and as I left the church I thought of the words Annie had spoken so often: 'Thank you for coming – come again,' and when we 'come again' to meet Annie in the great hereafter what a joyous greeting we will have.

CHAPTER XIV

EMMA

Strong and capable are words that come to mind when seeking words to describe her, and although these qualities were inherent in her nature, the hard reality of her early years had, I am sure, enhanced and strengthened them. Emma was my aunt, but much more – a mother, mentor and strict guardian of my morals and behaviour, to a degree which especially in my youth and teenage years, was, I am afraid, not always appreciated, although I loved her dearly. I realise now, that in the restrictions which I found irksome, she was motivated only by love and concern for my welfare.

The thatched cottage where Emma was born

Emma was born in 1870, one of twins, the other of which died at birth, and was the second eldest in a family of eleven children born to Ann Maria and Jeremiah Clarke – six boys and five girls living in a small Suffolk village – and life was hard.

One of her sisters, a little girl named Hannah, had died when only ten years old. She was operated on for appendicitis in their little overcrowded cottage, in circumstances that could have provided standards of hygiene far removed from what would be required today, and I suppose it would have been something of a miracle had she survived. Her mother was even allowed to be present in the room while the operation took place, and I have heard my grandmother describe her agonised feelings as she watched. One can imagine how traumatic and stressful this experience must have been for her, and indeed, the sad event was traumatic and overwhelming for all the family, for although one of many, Hannah had been greatly loved. The shock and circumstances of her death affected them all, her parents grieving for a much loved child and her siblings facing the reality of death, and at so early an age.

Emma's father, my grandfather Jeremiah, worked as a farm labourer for the local squire, who was also the rector of the parish church, and this ensured a life of servitude from which there was no escape. Any sign of discontent or rebellion would have meant the loss of both livelihood and home, for a tied cottage went with the job. It says much for his strength of character that he never allowed these circumstances to turn him into a servile individual. On the contrary, he was, as far as he could be, fiercely independent – this independence not easily achieved on a wage of ten shillings a week!

Although working long hours he, with great ingenuity, used every opportunity of finding means to provide for his large family. He sold honey from the bees which he kept and also produce from his garden, as well as keeping his household supplied with fresh vegetables and fruit. He was also the family's shoe mender, and woe betide any child found skipping, kicking stones or otherwise abusing freshly mended shoes – they could not afford to be thus used. It was his proud boast that it could never be said that the Clarke family owed anyone a halfpenny: not a mean feat in those days of hardship when state handouts were unknown. The only incident I ever heard of their receiving 'charity' was when occasionally the children were allowed to go to the 'big house' – the squire's – to be given a cup of dripping. In due time these precepts were instilled into his children and grandchildren, this strict adherence to honesty and independence it would seem almost becoming a dubious quality, as the following incident shows.

When, as a young boy, my brother was visiting my grandparents, he was sent on an errand to the village shop and, there being an odd halfpenny in the transaction, the kindly shopkeeper told him he could keep it for himself. His jubilation at this unexpected windfall, however, was short lived, as my grandfather, deciding that the halfpenny rightfully belonged to the shopkeeper, sternly told him to return it forthwith.

My grandmother, too, was perforce a woman of resource and ingenuity to enable her to feed and clothe her growing brood, and it was amazing that they all managed to grow strong and healthy with what we would consider today to be a far from balanced diet. What little meat they were able to afford was reserved for my grandfather

Jeremiah and Ann Maria with 9 of their 11 children.
Emma in top row, 4th from left

who certainly needed the sustenance to cope with his arduous life. I have heard Emma recount how, at a meal, the children were each allowed just two slices of bread, and if feeling still peckish they asked for more, they were sternly told, 'No, you've had your two slices.' On this bread allocation they were sometimes given slices of swede (their father's garden produce) which they would pretend was cheese!

Emma once told me how one year her mother, determined that the family would have meat for their Christmas dinner, had scrimped and saved for weeks beforehand in order to buy a joint to roast. On Christmas Eve the precious savings were handed to her mother's sister, who was entrusted to buy the eagerly awaited Christmas treat from the village butcher. But on her sister's return this joint, apparently, proved not to be at all up to the standard or size my grandmother had anticipated, and in her anger, disappointment and frustration, she flung the offending meat at the larder door, exclaiming, 'I on't hae'it.' (I won't have it) However, in the end she was forced to bow to the inevitable, and accepting the situation, and with practised and determined dexterity and ingenuity, managed, even with the less than acceptable meat, to give her family a good Christmas feast.

When at the end of the day the children were in bed, my grandmother's work was far from finished, for she then sewed buttonholes for the local clothing factory, for which she was paid the princely sum of one farthing per dozen! This work, of course, in the winter months all had to be done by candlelight; electricity and gas at that time were unknown in the village and oil for lamps was expensive. The factory was in operation for many years and was a source of full employment for those in the village not engaged in agriculture and enabled many of the women to supplement their husband's meagre wage by doing part-time work at home. The factory owners, aware of this need, were able to exploit the situation by paying abysmal wages for their hard-earned labours.

This, then, was the background in which Emma spent the early years of her life. My grandparents were determined that the children should receive what education was possible and that meant their finding one penny per week for each of them to attend the village school. This Emma did for five years. These were certainly years well spent, for during that time she acquired more learning and skills than many a child does today in twice as long a period, and with the advantage of modern schools and all that they can offer.

It says a lot, too, for the teachers of those days who had themselves probably overcome many difficulties to attain their position and would, by to-day's standards, be judged to have very inadequate teaching skills. Although at the end of those five years Emma's life was hard with very little time or opportunity to broaden her educational horizons, at the time that I knew her she had beautiful clear handwriting, her mathematical skills were sufficient to enable her to be an invaluable help to her husband in his business affairs, she wrote and spoke grammatically (and was, indeed, a gifted public speaker) and she took a lively and intelligent interest in local and national affairs.

At the age of ten Emma was judged to be old enough to earn her keep and was sent out to 'service'. This was necessary not only to relieve financial pressures, but because with the growing family, space in the cottage was at a premium.

Life in 'service' in the late nineteenth century was certainly no bed of roses. The demarcation line between the rich and poor was ever apparent and the class barrier never to be crossed. To the upper classes their menials were so taken for granted that, with few exceptions, their personalities, feelings or circumstances were an unknown quantity and they saw no reason to be concerned with them. Indeed the privileged classes would I am sure have been most surprised had their attitude and behaviour been called into question – it was the accepted norm. As far as they were concerned, if their servants came with good references and their work was satisfactory, they were fed and housed, provided with a uniform, and their wages (albeit meagre) paid regularly – thus their obligation towards them was fulfilled. It would not have occurred to them to make a point of seeing at first hand the conditions in which they worked, to view their cold and bare little shared attic bedrooms, or to concern themselves as to the suitability for immature young girls of the heavy work involved, for instance, of carrying coals up and down endless flights of stairs. Even had they made themselves cognisant of these facts, they would have been deemed normal conditions for the lower classes. In fact the servants would have been regarded as very fortunate to have been given the means of earning a livelihood.

The girls, too, of course, accepted these conditions as normal, conditions which would be totally unacceptable and horrifying to to-day's generation of young folk. Not only was a servant expected to be on duty for long hours at a stretch, but the work was physically demanding. For them there was a six o'clock, or even earlier, start to the day, so that everything should be in order and breakfast prepared when the household emerged from their slumbers some hours later. In the winter time this meant that after washing and dressing in their cold attic bedrooms (no central heating systems then!) there were grates to be cleaned and coal fires lit, rooms cleaned and tidied and breakfast prepared. In the larger households this work involved cooks, kitchen maids and housemaids. It was no leisurely operation; time was of the essence as most of those so busily engaged became invisible and retired to the servants' quarters before their employers put in an appearance. After their breakfast, of course, it was time to start on their next round of duties.

Some employers did, of course, show more consideration and generosity than others and when the girls, on their time off duty, met servants from other households, comparisons were exchanged and they would watch out for opportunities to better themselves. Below stairs it was very much an 'us' and 'them' situation and generally the girls, with good humour, high spirits and a sense of solidarity, would find their own ways of making life tolerable.

Emma's first place of service, at the age of ten, was with a family living some miles away from the village. Days off were few and far between and when they did occur meant a long, lonely walk along country roads to reach her home. On one occasion on setting out on the return journey she encountered a large noisy dog. Terrified, she ran back home, pleading to be allowed to stay. However, she realised her return was inevitable, and my grandfather, after calming her down, saw her on her way again. Emma learned at an early age to accept the inevitability of circumstances that cannot be changed!

Her life in service was a hard one for a girl of her tender years, having, as she did, to work long hours at tasks which would have proved onerous even for an adult. In later life she suffered considerably from flat feet, caused by carrying, in her formative years, heavy weights – young children and coals and logs for fires. She told me of many indignities and cruelties which, incredibly it seems, were, in those days, the norm for young girls to be subjected to. On one occasion when she let a knife slip and cut her arm, her mistress promptly rubbed a lump of cooking salt into the open wound, ignoring her screams and assuring her it was for her own good.

With one of her employers an arrangement was made whereby she was fed and clothed in lieu of wages. She, naturally, was not going to be clothed in style when her mistress could get away with dressing her in cheap materials and old cast-offs. So poor Emma was perforce to suffer many indignities during that period. Although all growing girls are sensitive about their appearance and it is important to them to look their best, with at least some concessions to the fashions of the day, for Emma that certainly was not taken into consideration. On one of her precious days off she arrived home unbecomingly attired in a dress of some coarse striped material, to be greeted by her young brothers with cries of, 'Here comes Emma in an old bed tick,' and maybe that is actually what it was, for at that time that was the kind of material used for covering mattresses! Imagine Emma's chagrin!

I think it was through those early experiences that Emma developed her strength and learned to hold her own in coping with life's problems. Even then, she did not take all the injustices lying down, incurring her mistress's displeasure as she occasionally made her feelings apparent. 'Don't look at me like that with those piercing brown eyes,' was a remark made to her by one mistress who had goaded her too far. It took a lot to quench that indomitable spirit. However, her protests must perforce always be guarded however much she longed to rebel against injustices, for the consequences would have been disastrous had she been dismissed from a post without references.

Gradually Emma began to realise that there was, outside her little world, a freedom of thought and outlook that she had not experienced in her life so far – a freedom from the servitude and injustices which her circumstances had imposed on her. These glimpses of independence and freedom were dawning on her horizon when, on one of her free days, she returned to the village home to visit her family. She and her mother were standing at their cottage gate when Mrs White, the rector's wife, happened to pass by in her carriage. Her mother, with due respect for 'her betters', made the customary curtsey as the carriage passed. Emma, however, greatly daring, refused to make this obeisance and stood her ground, much to her mother's surprise and consternation. 'Oh Emma,' she exclaimed, 'you den't bop t' Mrs White,' to which Emma, enjoying her new-found independence, daringly replied, 'No, I ain't a'gona pop t' she!'

In due course Emma began to feel that life might hold better prospects for her if she broadened her horizons. So in her early teens she took a post as kitchen maid in the racing community at Newmarket, where she came into contact with the young jockeys who were boarded there, and learned to hold her own coping with their banter and high spirits. When they were occasionally to get too fresh or to take liberties and make unwelcome advances, Emma's flashing brown eyes and firm rebuffs were usually effective in curbing their exuberance.

There was one occasion, however, when it appears that looks were not enough. One of the jockeys came up behind her in the kitchen, taking her unawares, and Emma, taken by surprise, lunged out at him with what happened to be in her hand at the time – a kitchen knife – with the result that he got a nasty cut on his hand. I don't know whether he or Emma was more surprised at what she had done. Horrified, Emma then bandaged his hand and they parted with no animosity between them. He, certainly, and the other jockeys and stable hands too, tended thereafter to treat Emma with more respect and their teasing became somewhat more tempered.

Having begun to spread her wings, Emma next went to work with a family at Southend-on-Sea in Essex, the first time she had ever left her native Suffolk. Her older brother George was at that time working on the railway which was then being built from London to Southend, and had met a certain Hector Carter who belonged to an old Wickford family. On one of Emma's free days George offered to introduce her to his friend Hector and that introduction was to set the course for the rest of her life. They started to 'walk out' and Emma fell in love with this handsome and attractive young man.

Hector, however, proved to be a bit of a ladies' man and inclined to 'play the field', which caused Emma some anxious moments and a bit of friction between them. Apparently she was not the only one to fall for his charms, so maybe it was not surprising that he, being flattered by so much attention from the fair sex, should sometimes succumb to the odd dalliance. As can be imagined this was not at all a satisfactory state of affairs as far as Emma was concerned.

Loyalty was high on her list of priorities as a necessary virtue in affairs of the heart, and anything less she was not prepared to accept. And so their courtship had its ups and downs, Hector seeming loth to make any firm commitment.

Things came to a head when one day, from the window of her employer's house, she saw her Hector strolling along with a pretty girl on his arm. He had, on occasion, when confronted with his dallyings, declared in defence of his actions, 'But it's only a bit of fun, you're the one I like best.' This was not good enough for her; she had to know where she stood, and this time she decided enough was enough. So Emma, the ever practical, delivered her ultimatum: either he promised to marry her and stop his philandering, or she would leave her employment and go away, out of his life forever. Knowing that Emma was not speaking idle words and faced with the prospect of losing her, Hector decided that she was indeed his true love and well worth sacrificing his 'bits of fun' for (a sensible decision on his part, it proved to be!) and thereafter a wedding was on the cards.

The way it was brought about, however, did give Hector a lever in the years that followed, jokingly to declare that Emma had been the one who proposed to him! – a forward thing for a girl to do in those days of strict protocol.

It must be said that this propensity for a harmless flirtation never left Hector, as Emma was aware, but it never threatened their marriage, which was to prove solid and enduring.

The marriage was arranged to take place on 2nd January 1892. No elaborate wedding for them! Money was scarce and what little they had managed to save was not to be squandered on unnecessary fripperies. Emma's parents were in no position to make the journey from Suffolk, having still a large family to care for and no money for railway fares. And so it came about that they were married quietly, with just two witnesses, on a snowy January day after walking together across the fields from the Carter family home to Wickford parish church. There was no thought of costly celebrations, and with no wedding guests to entertain, they returned, after the ceremony, to Hector's home, where his mother had prepared a meal of sausage and mash! The word honeymoon, I am sure, never entered their heads; such luxuries were not for the likes of them.

Their married life began in three furnished rooms in Southend-on-Sea. Hector worked as a bricklayer and resources were limited but Emma, ever resourceful and not afraid of hard work, proceeded to supplement their income by taking in washing – no washing machines or electric irons in those days to lighten her task. Now that she was established in her own home she began to make plans to help her family in Suffolk. There was work to be had in Southend and one by one her younger siblings were encouraged to come and seek their fortunes. Emma assumed the role of surrogate mother, looked after them and helped them to find work.

Until suitable work was found and they could establish themselves and become independent each one was provided with food and accommodation in the limited space of their new home. This could not have been easy, but Emma, with her resourcefulness and management skills, and Hector's support, saw that the arrangement worked, and her parents were relieved of any anxieties about the welfare of their brood.

When it was my father's turn to leave the Suffolk home he managed to find work on a farm in the village of Barling, some five miles distant from Southend, and there met my mother. This meeting apparently caused some consternation to my mother's parents – that this strange young man from unknown Suffolk should come courting their daughter! After all she was very young and inexperienced in the ways of the world, and of him they knew nothing. However, their fears proved to be unfounded, for eventually Joseph and Emily married, stayed in the village and raised their family, of which I am one!

Thus it was, with the gradual migration from Suffolk, that the Clarke family came to be established in the Southend area.

Hector, through dint of hard work, enterprise and initiative, and with Emma's loyal support and encouragement, eventually established his own business as a builder. This was, indeed, some achievement, as his formal education had been sparse, and yet I never knew him to employ an accountant – and rarely an architect. To keep accounts and draw up plans for all the houses he built was no mean achievement. Besides coping with the brain work he always worked alongside his employees, putting in long hours as a skilled bricklayer. Admittedly, running a business was not fraught with the hazards and complications that it is to-day; nevertheless, it says a lot for his character and capabilities that for many years he ran a successful business, and many of the houses in Southend are to-day proof of his good workmanship and skill.

In all this Emma played her part, bearing with him when things were not going too well and lending a sympathetic ear and sharing his anxieties when sales were slow and the cash was not forthcoming for further building to be proceeded with. In practical ways too he could always rely on her help. I well remember our Friday afternoon visits to the bank where, as a young child, I regularly accompanied her to collect the men's weekly wages. Indeed I looked forward to the adventure of our weekly bus rides, and on arriving at the bank to watch the sovereigns and half sovereigns being scooped up in a little brass shovel and placed on the counter scales. No sophisticated technology in those days and no fear of muggers as we proceeded home carrying the cash.

Throughout many years Emma was the mainstay of the family; whenever any member was in trouble or need, or seeking advice, it was to her that they turned, relying on her dependability and readiness to step in wherever she was needed. Ever practical, her advice was listened to and her help gratefully accepted. This help, although given unstintingly, was often at great cost. Not only was monetary assistance sometimes involved, but often also much labour and devotion. One of Hector's nieces, who had lost her mother when very young, was promptly taken into their home and was lovingly cared for until she married and had children of her own who were in turn also recipients of their love and concern.

By the time I was born Emma was no longer young. My mother already had two children and was not in the best of health, so when as a small baby I developed infantile eczema, she found it hard to cope. This was when Emma once more stepped into the breach and, without more ado, took me into her home and undertook the formidable task of caring for this ailing infant. This undertaking might well even have daunted a much younger and caring parent, for the situation required round the clock vigilance and care. It was a weeping eczema which covered my head, face and limbs, causing constant discomfort and irritation. I could not be washed normally and had to be oiled and bandaged and rebandaged at frequent intervals. At night my hands were gloved and tied down to prevent my scratching the eruption, and I remember Emma telling me how one night I managed to get a hand free and she woke to find me in a sorry state with my face covered in blood where I had rubbed the skin raw. So besides all the extra work involved there was a very fretful child to contend with.

To have undertaken this marathon task for a child who was not her own says a lot, I think, for Emma's caring and compassionate nature as well as her stamina and strength. Although all kinds of medical help and advice was sought, the condition persisted until I had cut my teeth, so this hard labour, coupled with anxiety and lack of sleep, was no short-term commitment.

This period of their married life reveals also Hector's generous and caring nature in that he never begrudged Emma the time and attention given to me, which must have really taken over a large part of her life at that time. Indeed she always had his support and they were one in sympathy and care which they unstintingly lavished upon me. Hector loved children and was always happy in their company. I remember the happy times we had when, as a small child, he would take me on his knee and tell me stories or we would explore the delights of his large illustrated encyclopaedia or a favourite picture book. It always remained a great disappointment to them that they had no children of their own.

During this time Emma was concerned that I should not lose contact with my mother and, at frequent intervals, wheeled me in my pram to visit my family in the village of Wakering, some five miles distant. The round trip of ten miles, after a disturbed night and the work and time entailed in getting me ready for the journey, was, obviously, no mean undertaking.

I have letters written to my mother at that time, in which Emma expresses compassion and concern for my plight and understanding for my mother in being parted from her child, but never a word of complaint about the part she was playing. She was at pains that my mother should have no anxiety about my well being, assuring her that I was receiving loving care and the best of attention.

At the age of five I had grown into a healthy and happy child. My skin was completely clear and my hair had grown thick and golden. It was no wonder then that both Hector and Emma took delight in this child in whom there was such a transformation due to their care and attention and whom they had grown to love dearly. It was then

The author aged 4 years outside 'Mow Cop' with pram and teddy bear

77

that my mother decided that I should go back to live in the family home, where there was an elder brother and sister. Emma and Hector, although devastated at the prospect of giving me up, knew this was what they had to do. This decision, the implementation of which was sudden and with very little warning, caused heartbreak both for them and for me. I found it very hard and bewildering to be uprooted from the security of their loving home and having to adjust to living with a family I hardly knew, especially as my mother decided that in the circumstances of living as an only child I had been 'spoiled' and that discipline was of paramount importance! This traumatic experience affected my life in many ways. I did, however, go back to live with Hector and Emma when I started secondary school education and remained close to them for the rest of their lives.

Emma was a devout Christian, but hers was no 'pie-in-the-sky' religion; it was an essential part of her and was lived out and motivated all her actions. Practical by nature, Emma was ever ready to go into action and practise what she preached. However, with all her propensity for loving and caring this did not normally extend to the animal kingdom – or, at least she preferred to do her loving and caring from a distance! She was firmly convinced that animals and humans should not share the same habitation: the place for animals was definitely outside the home. Especially she could not tolerate cats; she was never happy in their presence and had a real aversion to coming into contact with their furry coats. At one point Hector and I tried to overcome her objections and (very unadvisedly, as I see now) introduced into our home a small ginger kitten, hoping that she would eventually come to tolerate it. Her distaste for the poor little creature was very apparent. After handling the kitten I was not allowed to touch or prepare any food until I had thoroughly washed my hands and all its feeding bowls had to be kept well away from anything which we were likely to use. It was a very trying time for poor Emma, and indeed for us all, and when, at the age of three months, my little Joe died from cat flu, Emma's equanimity was restored and our household returned to some semblance of normality. However I mourned my little cat, the only pet I was ever able to keep from then on.

In spite of this aversion Emma's instincts prevailed when practical help was needed for a member of the animal kingdom – yes, even for a cat, as you will see from the following incident – and for which help she received scant reward. I came home from work one day to find Emma looking a sorry sight, with her face covered in violet coloured scratches. In some consternation I enquired, 'What has done this?' and to my surprise she replied grimly, 'A cat!' It transpired that a neighbour had called saying that a cat was stranded in a nearby tree, crying piteously and unable to get down. Being Emma, she, of course, promptly went to see if she could help, and while standing under the tree trying to entice the cat down, it had suddenly taken a flying leap, landing on poor Emma as it scrambled down and fled the scene. The neighbour, seeking to mitigate potential resultant harm from the scratches which had been inflicted, had painted them with iodine – what ironies life holds!

Their home, as I remember it from my early childhood, was warm, harmonious and hospitable. In those early days Hector, ever energetic, did an early morning stint on the building site and, as a small child, I would slip into Emma's bed and await the cup of tea he always brought up before going to work. (By that time we were living in one of the houses that Hector had built.) On winter mornings Emma would have a lovely blazing fire going by the time he came home, and I can well remember his cheery greeting as Emma busily prepared our breakfast. Yes, my early impressions of that home were indeed of warmth, security and contentment.

Later on, after my grandfather Jeremiah died, my grandmother was brought from her Suffolk cottage to live with us, and was given every consideration, being lovingly cared for by both Emma and Hector alike. Then, after a time, Hector's ageing mother joined the household, resulting in a ménage which one might have thought would be a situation fraught with difficulties. But surprisingly there was never any friction. The old ladies got along splendidly and enjoyed each other's company, no doubt having much in common as they discussed their experiences in bringing up their respective families. Emma and Hector loved them both dearly and spared no effort in ensuring their welfare. This love was reciprocated and they, in their turn, made their contribution in making a happy and harmonious household. Although the house was small, they were provided with every comfort, each having her own armchair by the fire, and as far as possible their every wish being granted. In today's climate one can hardly imagine these household arrangements being contemplated, let alone proving a success. But it worked, mainly, I think, through Emma's efforts and the calm and peaceful environment she created.

Although Emma's formal education had ended after five years attendance at the village school, her intellectual interest in life and people had been a great educator. She was an avid reader when time permitted, often staying up to read after the rest of the household had retired, and was able to absorb and retain the knowledge she gained. She wrote a beautiful and clear hand and the basic grammar and arithmetic acquired so young stood her in good stead, so much so that she was of invaluable help to her husband in dealing with his business transactions. At this time she also got much enjoyment from playing the piano which had been recently purchased. She had had no formal tuition, but a friend having taught her the notes from a musical score, she persevered until she could creditably play the hymn tunes which she loved. That same piano was the one on which I, my daughter and my granddaughter learned to play, and which I still have in my possession.

Emma had had connections with Methodism from her early days in the Suffolk village of her childhood, although my grandfather, being an employee and entirely dependent on the local squire and rector for his home and livelihood, was expected to attend, with his family, the Anglican parish church. However, the children, surreptitiously and always in fear of being found out, would go along to the little Primitive Methodist chapel on special occasions, such as the Sunday School Anniversary – a big event in the village life – my grandmother having instructed them not to let anyone from 'the big house' see them going in. Having to pass the rectory to reach the chapel their strategy was to crawl along under the hedge until they were sure of not being seen. Such was the power and authority of the squire and clergy in those days. So, on coming to live in Southend Emma and Hector gravitated to and became members of a local Primitive Methodist Church.

The world wide Methodist Church, as it is to-day, was founded in the early eighteenth century by John Wesley, an Anglican clergyman who, after a profound religious experience, was fired with a burning zeal to proclaim the gospel of Christianity. This desire to take the gospel to the common people outside the confines of church buildings and his enthusiasm for social reform brought him into disfavour with the traditional Anglican Church, and finally to his severance from it, although this was always a great grief to him and had never been his intention. He achieved so much in his lifetime, facing persecution and all manner of hazards as he travelled on horseback to all parts of the British Isles. It is said he rode 5,000 miles a year, and when he died in 1791 had covered a quarter of a million miles in his lifetime – a similar distance as from the earth to the moon!

In the wake of Wesley's visits, mostly to the rural areas of Britain, little groups of worshippers began to meet in cottages and small homesteads and then, as his influence grew, places of worship began to be built. Then followed the necessity for some kind of co-ordination, involving administration and rules of procedure. Lay preaching was sanctioned, a court of discipline and cabinet of administration formed. Groups of churches were formed into 'Circuits', Wesley appointing Superintendents for each Circuit. Circuit horses were acquired, making it possible for each Superintendent to visit all his churches, some Circuits being fifty miles in extent. We are told that books, provisions and *spades* were carried on these journeys, the roads, in the winter, often turning into quagmires and drastic action being needed to extricate the horses and travellers. Of all the hazards encountered, highwaymen were not often a cause for concern, for they knew that from travelling preachers there was never money to steal! Actually they were paid the princely sum of £3 per quarter. With the rapid growth of the movement and the growing need for administration and organisation, an annual conference took place, the first being held in 1744. Thus Methodism came into being.

Historians claim that Wesley and Methodism saved England from the horrors of a revolution. It has been said: 'You cannot detach him from our national life: no single figure influenced so many minds, no single voice touched so many hearts; no other man did such a life work for England.'

During those early years many different types of people were attracted to Wesley's preaching and teaching. The Quakers at one time had strong links with Methodism and also William Booth who later founded the Salvation Army. As the movement developed it was inevitable that there should be differing opinions on questions of procedures and forms of worship. In the early eighteen hundreds some felt that the church was losing some of its early evangelical zeal, becoming too stereotyped and the form of worship too liturgical. It was felt that the early enthusiasm which prompted Wesley to take the message to the people outside the confines of church buildings was being lost.

Such were the views of two very different characters, Hugh Bourne and William Clowes who, because of their very strong convictions, broke away from the original Methodist Church, and in 1807 formed what came to be known as the Primitive Methodist Church, the branch of Methodism to which, a century later, Emma and Hector gave their allegiance.

Hugh Bourne, born in 1772, left school at eleven years of age and learned the trades of wheelwright and carpenter, but also spent many hours studying Hebrew, Greek, Latin, Astronomy and Philosophy. He was somewhat shy and dour and lived simply, but he was disciplined and courageous in putting his beliefs into practice.

William Clowes, however – born in 1780, and a potter by trade – had an emotional and magnetic personality. He was vigorous and energetic and had experienced a dynamic conversion to Christianity with rapid spiritual growth.

In this new Church rules were democratically made and besides a new freedom to vary methods of worship, one of the main features of Primitive Methodism became the holding of open air meetings, which came to be known as Camp Meetings, the first of which was held on 31st May 1807 on Mow Cop hill in Staffordshire. This was an all-day event to which people came from far and wide.

There was a certain amount of opposition to the new methods of this Church and persecution followed. Cottagers who sheltered travelling preachers or lent their homes for services risked losing their homes or their employment. Farmers suffered as stocks of precious grain and farm buildings were set alight. In the early 1800s John Wedgewood was pulled down while preaching at the Market Cross in a Midland town, and led off to prison. At Newark a Mr Lockwood had the town's fire engine hose played upon him as though he was on fire, and while half drowned he gurgled, 'You can't quench the fire within!' Church bells and brass bands were requisitioned to drown the voice of preachers. Even courts of law were hard on these Christians and in 1830 a man named Russell was sentenced to three months hard labour for selling hymn books and magazines. But in spite of all opposition these Camp Meetings survived until well into the twentieth century. What a life-changing faith these early Methodists possessed!

As a child in the village where my parents lived our lives revolved around the Primitive Methodist chapel and its activities, and these Camp Meetings were a highlight in the church calendar. Whit Sunday was the main Camp Meeting day, and a joyful occasion it was too. It involved the whole circuit of churches, and preachers would come from the surrounding area to take part, making a day of it and being given hospitality by the local church members. As children, not knowing much outside the life of the village, we found it exciting to entertain in our home these visiting preachers from unknown territory!

In the morning, after meeting in the chapel we would proceed through the village, making various halts, at each of which the scriptures would be read, prayers offered and a 'message' given by one of the visiting preachers. Hector revelled in the Camp Meeting days and was always in great demand, as his stentorian tones could be guaranteed to penetrate even into the surrounding cottages!

We carried with us a small portable harmonium, which was set up at each stop. No Methodist gathering was complete without Wesley hymns, and how those Methodists could sing! After lunch these meetings would continue with a different set of preachers taking part, and in the evening we gathered in the chapel for the annual 'Love Feast'. This was a service in which members of the congregation were invited to participate, sharing their religious experiences and testifying to the transforming power of God in their lives. At the end of the meeting an invitation was given for anyone to come and kneel at the 'penitent form', confess their sins, confirm their faith and promise to lead a new life. As a small child I remember confusing a Love Feast with a church social and asking my father if the Love Feast was where we had tea and cakes. He explained, with some amusement, that the latter was not 'that kind of feast'! This meeting tended to become very emotional, some of the congregation weeping tears of joy as they saw hitherto non-Christians responding to the love of God. I remember I found this very disturbing and, as I grew older, anticipated the Whit Sunday Love Feast with some discomfiture. But it was the culmination of Camp Meeting Sunday, a truly great day which had an impact on many lives, including those of Emma and Hector.

On 31st May 1907 Centenary celebrations were held on Mow Cop hill in Staffordshire, the site of the first Camp Meeting, and it was Emma and Hector's great delight to attend these celebrations. Holidays at that time were an unknown luxury for them, and this break from routine on such a special occasion was, indeed, a highlight in their lives; every detail of this wonderful event was impressed upon their minds for many years to come.

Many years later I happened, quite by chance, to find in a second-hand shop a plate made in Burslem to commemorate this centenary. Apparently there were two editions of this plate and mine was the first edition made. Over a picture of the castle on Mow Hill, where the first Camp Meeting was held, are the words: 'The little cloud increaseth still which first arose upon Mow Hill.' Three Staffordshire Primitive Methodist chapels are also depicted, at Tunstall, Burslem and Mow Cop, and in the centre, pictures of Hugh Bourne and William Clowes with the dates of their birth and death. On the back of the plate are interesting details headed 'What God has wrought!', showing the number of chapels, Ministers, local preachers, church members, adherents, Sunday Schools, teachers, scholars and also the value of property owned at that time – £4,958,978.

You may imagine Emma and Hector's delight when I arrived home with this precious find. It was highly treasured during their lifetime and is in my possession to-day.

Our house was named 'Mow Cop' and this fact one day brought an unexpected experience into our lives in the shape of a con-man.

He arrived at our door out of the blue, claiming to be interested in the name 'Mow Cop' and asking if we were Primitive Methodists. This was enough to ensure him a welcome into our home. What his connection with the Church was we never knew but he was very well informed and most knowledgeable on the subject and history of Primitive Methodism, and, needless to say, Emma and Hector were delighted to meet a fellow enthusiast and have the opportunity to talk on their favourite topic of conversation. He was invited to stay for a meal – to which he did good justice – during which he told us of the large estate which he owned in Scotland, and which we were invited to visit as his guests. Oh yes, he was very plausible! He then informed us that he had urgent business to attend to there and was planning to make the overnight journey home. Hector then offered to escort him to the station and on the way was regaled with a tale of how he came to be short of ready cash. Hector, confident

Emma outside 'Mow Cop' with author aged 4

85

that a good Primitive Methodist could be nothing less than honest, then 'loaned' him his fare to Scotland. Where he had come from and where he went with the cash we never knew, but that was the last we heard of him!

The church which Emma and Hector attended on coming to Southend-on-Sea was a large building situated near to the sea front. Hector's background had been somewhat different from Emma's and, at the time of their marriage, having sown a few 'wild oats', he had had very little connection with church life. However, he attended the services with Emma and, under her influence and that of the church, experienced a religious conversion and became a committed Christian. Radical changes in his life had to be made. The Church at that time required its members to become teetotal and frowned on their indulging in the smoking of tobacco. So Hector became teetotal, but found relinquishing his beloved pipe a hard sacrifice to make. However, Emma, with her strong faith, had the solution. 'Go upstairs,' she told him, 'get down on your knees and ask the Lord to take away the *desire*.' This Hector did and it worked! The pipe was thrown into the fire and from that time no alcohol was allowed to enter our house or tobacco smoked therein! Indeed this reversal almost became an obsession with him, causing him to become somewhat condemnatory and intolerant of others.

His brother, who had a taste for smoking small cheroots, sometimes came to visit us. Poor Horace, knowing that he dare not offend Hector by smoking in the house had, perforce, to retreat to the outside loo to enjoy his little cheroots!

The Church's teaching and their strong beliefs determined their code of behaviour, which required them to become 'unworldly', not socialising at dances, for instance, or visiting cinemas or theatres (restrictions which, as I grew older, I found irksome and unreasonable). At that time television and even the radio had not entered our homes and so our whole lives centred around the church and its activities. Both Emma and Hector were unquestionably loyal to their church to which they gave unstintingly of their time, money and talents.

The keeping of the Sabbath was strictly observed, the focus of course being the Sunday services, usually three every Sunday. But the observance did not end there: the whole day, as far as possible, must be kept 'holy'; the Bible's instruction that 'six days shalt thou labour' was strictly followed, and only essentials in the way of work were done. The mid-day meal was always a cold one – cooking was unnecessary work! And I can still see the pile of dishes from the mid-day meal stacked neatly on the draining board ready to be tackled on Monday morning. But it was by no means a gloomy day and only 'holy' in the best sense of the word. The church services were happy and joyful occasions and as a child I enjoyed this special day when we could spend it happily together as a family – Hector being at home with us was a bonus! It was different and looked forward to with joyous anticipation.

Church teas were popular, usually preceded or followed by a religious gathering. Here the ladies' culinary skills were brought to bear in preparing and serving the food. Emma's practical skills certainly came to the fore when it came to fund-raising efforts. I have memories of being lulled to sleep by the hum of her sewing machine as she stitched endless garments to be sold at the church bazaars. These were great social occasions and looked forward to with much anticipation in the days when our lives had little in the way of entertainment. Occasions such as a bazaar would be supported by other churches on the Methodist Circuit, and so would give us an opportunity to meet up with friends and acquaintances who otherwise we would rarely see.

During these years both Hector and Emma became lay preachers and travelled round the circuit of Methodist Churches, conducting services in Southend and its environs. Bus services to the outlying towns and villages were practically non-existent and most of the local preachers relied on their bicycles for transport or even walked many miles in all weathers to keep their preaching appointments. At that time most of the Primitive Methodist Churches (chapels, as they were known in the villages) held two or even three services each Sunday and so the preachers would make a day of it and be given hospitality by the church members. As a child I always looked forward to the Sundays when we entertained the visiting preachers, who came bringing a bit of the outside world into the village and into our homes.

This situation posed a problem for Emma, as she had never mastered the art of riding a bicycle. However, this was an obstacle to be overcome and, nothing daunted, she became the proud possessor of a tricycle. So, with Hector on his bicycle and Emma secure on her three wheels, they often set out together to keep their various preaching appointments. Later, with more traffic on the roads, their journeys proved more hazardous and the rare sight of a bus on the road caused Emma some consternation. On a country road one Sunday morning Emma was surprised and somewhat startled to hear a bus approaching from behind, and looked round to see exactly how near it was. In doing so she inadvertently turned the handlebars and steered her tricycle into the wayside ditch. Fortunately it was dry and she climbed out unscathed except for scratches sustained from the bramble hedge against which she had fallen, and, shaken but undaunted, proceeded on her way. I imagine her congregation were somewhat surprised to see, in their pulpit, a slightly dishevelled figure, her countenance showing the marks of her encounter with the brambles!

These stalwarts served as lay preachers in the Methodist Church for well over fifty years and I have in my possession certificates presented to them on their having given fifty years service.

I have said the marriage was solid; so it was and I think nothing could have jeopardised it. However, as Emma discovered prior to their marriage, Hector was a ladies' man and this fact was to cause Emma some concern in the years that followed. As a young man Hector was handsome with an attractive personality and he loved feminine company, so I suppose it was inevitable that the young ladies in the church circles in which they moved should also be attracted to him. It followed that he was often surrounded by a circle of young ladies who enjoyed his company. Some of these young people would often accompany Emma and Hector home from church on Sunday mornings and it would be Hector's delight to show them around his garden, which was his pride and joy, where there would be much lively laughter and light hearted banter, while Emma would be away in the kitchen preparing lunch for us.

The situation was exacerbated when Emma's mother came to live with us. She found it hard to adjust when uprooted from her village home and in her insecurity was unwilling to be left in the house alone. This, of course, restricted Emma's movements and she was unable to accompany Hector to many of their church activities. If, on occasion, Emma remonstrated with Hector on the wisdom of his behaviour he was always surprised at her concern, saying, 'But matey, you know there's nothing wrong in it, it's all just a bit of fun.' And I'm sure this was true and, at its worst, the whole thing just mildly flirtatious. Emma rarely acknowledged she found it a problem and said very little; her loyalty to Hector was absolute and neither by word nor deed would she let her concerns be known. But I know she was often hurt and maybe a little jealous to think that he should prefer others' company to her own. Hector, of course, fell prey to the flattery and popularity which he engendered, but he knew Emma's worth, relied on her strengths and loved her too dearly to wish to hurt her. This time she could

Emma and Hector with Hector's niece

give him no 'ultimatum', and I think he never really knew the extent of her concern and the hurts which she silently bore.

Few people knew Emma intimately. She was a woman of few words and rarely expressed her thoughts, or indeed indulged in idle chatter. When hearing her preach or speak in public I would marvel at the depth of thought expressed, of which I had no inkling as in the preceding days we had been coping with the practicalities of life together. She had always been, physically, very strong and healthy and she found it hard to feel empathy for physical weakness. But when she encountered it her sympathy, although rarely expressed, was evident in her instant response to a call for practical help. This reserve, and her somewhat stern demeanour, tended to prevent acquaintances from seeing the true Emma and sometimes caused her to be misunderstood. This exterior which others saw was very different from the Emma whom I knew and loved. The depths of her nature were revealed to very few, but once she had given her love or allegiance it never wavered; she was to be completely trusted and relied upon – a rare quality.

Someone said of early Methodism, 'It is a potent mixture of deep personal faith – dynamic and life-changing – and a commitment to radical social action. Looking at its various branches we see a great church (or set of churches), one in doctrine, one in aim, one in life, divided only or mainly by forms of government and details of discipline.'

The year 1932 brought about a big change in Methodism; it was the year of Methodist Union, when three branches of that great church, the Wesleyans, the Primitives, and the Free Church joined together to become the Methodist Church. No longer was it 'divided by forms of government and details of discipline'.

It was inevitable that there should be problems with all the massive reorganisation involved, and compromises had to be made. In towns and villages where two denominations had been worshipping separately – mainly Wesleyans and Primitives – it followed that, to achieve unity, one of the church buildings had to be closed. The Wesleyans, at that time, were the stronger denomination, both numerically and financially, the Wesleyan church often being the larger building. And so it was that many former Primitive Methodist churches were closed. Understandably, this was not always easy to accept as far as the former 'Prims' were concerned; they sometimes felt that rather than 'uniting' they were being absorbed by the more predominant church. They tended to find the form of worship rather more formal and less evangelical in the former Wesleyan churches and, especially in the villages where the lives of several generations had revolved round a particular church, the transition was not easy. Certainly adjustments and compromises had to be made.

This merger was to make a major change in the lives of Emma and Hector. Anxious as they were to retain their Primitive Methodist identity they viewed the question of 'Unity' with some misgivings. These apprehensive forebodings were time and again voiced in the circuit meetings where the subject was discussed and when 'Union' eventually became a reality they were dismayed to find that their beloved church, to which they had given so many years of devoted service, was on the closure list. They, together with other church members who strongly deprecated this move, tried hard to dissuade the church authorities from carrying out their intention. Many meetings and private discussions took place, where feelings ran high. It affected our home life, where this dire threat hung over us like a cloud.

Hector, especially, was determined that they should not lose their 'spiritual home', and that the lovely building should not be sold (as was proposed) and fall into secular use. As time went on and it was becoming apparent that they were fighting a losing battle, a majority of the 'opposers' gave up the fight and were prepared to cede their cause. This, however, Hector, with tenacity and albeit some obstinacy, was not prepared to do. As a trustee of the church his consent was vital as the agreement of all the trustees was necessary to bring about a closure. So, all the other trustees having eventually given their consent, Hector became the only obstacle in the way of the proposed plan. Thus he became a very unpopular figure with the church authorities.

This became a very traumatic time in our family, the situation dominating all thought and conversation. It was also a very unhappy time as Emma and Hector contemplated with real grief what this loss would mean to them. The problem became the concern of the

91

church hierarchy beyond the jurisdiction of the circuit and I remember meetings taking place where high ranking church officials were using all their persuasive powers in order that their plans could proceed.

With all this pressure being brought to bear the situation became impossible and in the end Hector had to bow to the inevitable and sign the necessary document which was to sever their last links with Primitive Methodism. Even so, he was to insist on one last concession – that before being sold, the spire should be removed from the church building. Although it was agreed, this was never carried out and I believe remains in place to this day. When sold, the building was turned into a factory which produced Southend rock. Visitors strolling along the seafront today with their sticks of Southend rock might be surprised to learn of the cost and heartache which led to its production!

They did eventually accept the new order and joined one of the 'merger' churches, where they gave loyal service for many years to come.

Before Hector retired he decided they should move into a somewhat larger house and bought some land just a few yards from their existing home. Emma, on being asked her preferences for her new home, made two stipulations. First she wanted to live in the front of the house, where she could see some life, having previously always lived with a back garden outlook. Secondly she wanted the living room to be spacious with room to move around (space had previously been at a premium when, at times, their home had become somewhat overcrowded). So Hector, in building the house, complied with her wishes, and the large room became the scene of many happy family gatherings, especially over the Christmas season; it also provided the venue for my wedding reception, where Emma brought all her organising and catering skills to bear!

On retiring at the age of sixty, Hector bought a small car and learned to drive and during the following years they were able to enjoy some well deserved leisure. This little car was to give them a hitherto unexperienced freedom to visit family and friends scattered around East Anglia and to enjoy the beauties of the countryside in their travels. This joy they were always willing to share with others.

Cars were not so commonly owned as they are today and it was their delight to invite friends and acquaintances to join them on these excursions. Many a housebound acquaintance had reason to be grateful for their thoughtfulness in providing them with a welcome brief release from their four walls.

At that time Emma was very much in demand as a speaker at Church Women's Meetings in Southend and the surrounding district and on these occasions Hector was happy to play the part of chauffeur. He would often take a book, park outside the hall and enjoy a read until the meeting was over. He grew to be a familiar figure on meeting days and would not be forgotten when the inevitable cup of tea was brewed! Emma continued to carry on this voluntary service until well into her eighties.

When they reached their Golden Wedding Anniversary, war time restrictions and shortages made suitable celebrations impossible. Ten years on, however, their Diamond Wedding was happily celebrated by a large gathering of family and friends. The church hall was hired and they were surprised to hear a recording of the Wedding March played as they were greeted by their guests. At the celebratory meal both Emma and Hector spoke with thankfulness of their long life together and expressed their joy at meeting all their relatives and friends who had come to celebrate with them. Various folk entertained during the evening and Emma recited a lengthy poem which she had learned many years before – a remarkable feat of memory! It was a truly happy occasion, but needless to say an entirely teetotal one!

Emma faced the limitations and restrictions of the advancing years with a typically philosophical and stoical attitude, although increasing inactivity could not have been easy to accept. As she had become less mobile she had taken up embroidery as a hobby although hitherto her sewing skills had been used for more practical purposes. This new hobby gave her much pleasure and she spent many happy hours creating articles of usefulness and beauty, which found their way into the homes of friends and relatives. When, as her eyesight began to fail and her stitching became less than perfect, she was forced to give up her enjoyable pastime, I never once heard her complain or express any regret as she calmly put aside her silks and accepted the inevitable.

Emma and Hector both lived into their nineties, Emma's unselfish prayer being answered that she should outlive her spouse; Hector had always been reliant on her and needed her strengths and her wish was to be there for him as long as he needed her. In her eighties she had suffered a stroke from which she fully recovered, but during her illness Hector was completely devastated; she had always been so strong and he found it hard to come to terms with the possibility of facing life without her. As she grew frail in her latter years her mind remained alert and active and she retained an intelligent interest in topical and world affairs. Her hearing was unimpaired and, after Hector died, she relied a lot on her little radio for company. She had tended to go along with his choice of programme, but now she chose for herself and this was a great source of interest for her. It was a link with the outside world. She enjoyed a variety of programmes – on which she formed her own decided opinions! – but, no longer being able to attend church, the religious topics and church services were a priority.

By this time all her siblings had passed on and I am sure she must have felt a loneliness to be the only family member of her generation left, especially when she had been so involved with the welfare of them all. But never once did I hear her complain, neither of her physical limitations, nor of her circumstances.

Emma celebrated her ninety-fourth birthday with a party of family and friends in her 'large' room. As the cake was cut and the candles extinguished she rose to her feet and made what was to be her final speech, thanking her guests for coming and those who had organised her party. Then, with what one wonders may have been some prescience of the future, she expressed her hope that we would all join her in the Heaven which her strong faith had made for her such a shining certainty. Within a week of that celebration Emma had made that transition, being spared the weariness of a long illness, which would have robbed her of the independence which, all her life, had been such an essential part of her.

I feel that Emma and Hector's influence for good reached far beyond the bit of world that they knew, for on their journey through life their influence on the lives they touched and their contribution to the happiness and well-being of many will be long remembered. What more fitting epitaph could there be than the words inscribed on their tombstone: 'Well done thou good and faithful servants.'

CHAPTER XV

JOSEPH

Joseph was my father, an unremarkable man some would have said, but I suppose every individual is remarkable in his own way, and Joseph was no exception – a quiet man, yes, and unobtrusive, but he certainly had his strengths, and mine was definitely not the only life on which he left his mark.

Joseph belonged to the Clarke family and was the brother of Emma, of whom I have also written. He was a countryman born and bred and never had any desire to live in the fast lane. Being brought up in humble circumstances, one of a large family, he had never known material wealth and, indeed, I think never desired it. But it could never be said that he was poor in the things that mattered, and certainly not 'poor in spirit'. He was a humble man, humble in the best sense of the word – for surely humility is a sign of greatness – but never servile.

When as a young man Joseph moved to Essex from his native Suffolk, he found employment as a cowman with a local farmer. It was then that he had an unfortunate encounter with a bull. Too late he saw the bull moving menacingly towards him and although he ran, could not reach the gate before it caught up with him and knocked him to the ground. Knowing that he could not escape, he lay looking up at the animal as it stood over him. After what must have seemed like an eternity the bull evidently decided that he had made his conquest, lost interest and ambled away, much to Joseph's relief. As a child I remember listening with horror and fascination as my father recounted this adventure and was ever after very wary when crossing country meadows.

In the village he began to attend the small Methodist chapel, and there he met my mother. There was instant mutual attraction and they soon began 'walking out'. This development caused my maternal grandparents much consternation. This Joseph Clarke was an unknown quantity – a foreigner from far away Suffolk! Moreover, Emily their daughter was only eighteen and this stranger a man of twenty-five! It was rare in those days for girls to marry outside their village and so, in the circumstances, Joseph was suspect; but not for long. He was able to win their confidence, and a year later they were married in the village parish church.

Their first child, a baby boy, sadly died a few days after birth. This was a great grief to them and very hard to come to terms with, especially so as my mother always felt that the baby might have lived had not the doctor called to the birth arrived in a drunken and incompetent state. However, life has to go on and they were eventually blessed with four more children, of whom I was the third.

Joseph worked hard and conscientiously all his life to care for his family, although in the process never achieving fame or fortune. As I think of the vicissitudes of his life, it is his quietness, gentleness and patience with which he faced every situation, which I remember

Joseph and Emily's wedding photo. Emma is standing on far right.

as an essential part of him. He was a man of few words, but when spoken these were generally relevant, to the point and full of sense and wisdom. They also revealed a depth of thought not apparent to many.

Joseph always saw the best in people, even when that best was hard to find. I think I never heard him say anything unkind or derogatory about anyone, nor did he encourage his family to do so. But he certainly had a sense of humour – a very dry humour and wit, which popped out at unexpected moments. He was quick to see the ridiculous and inappropriateness in people and situations, and although he would enjoy a quiet chuckle at their expense it was never hurtful and certainly not malicious.

He was also a man of peace; disharmony among friends or in the home was an anathema to him, although he would never have compromised his principles to gain it. This trait in his character was not always appreciated by his family. My mother, who was always the dominant force in the partnership, sometimes became rather

Joseph and Emily with their three youngest children, the author standing on left.

99

frustrated when she felt that peace should not have been the chief factor in solving a situation. She was by way of being a disciplinarian and was inclined to take the view that my father should have given her more support when it came to disciplining the children. There was, in consequence, occasionally a difference of opinion between them when my father, in the pursuit of peace, was inclined to overlook some minor misdemeanour, and my mother was convinced that more stringent methods of dealing with the matter should be applied.

I remember an occasion in my early teens when my elder brother and I were planning a trip to Wales, with me riding pillion on his motorbike. When this came to my mother's ears she was horrified (maybe justifiably!) and promptly vetoed the whole idea. My father appeared to have no strong objection, but when appealed to for his approval, made it clear that we must not oppose my mother's decision. He knew well, of course, that had he given his permission it would have caused friction between him and my mother, and he would do nothing deliberately to cause disharmony between them. I remember saying to my brother at the time, 'I think Dad is just *too* peace-loving.' My brother, of course, was allowed to go and I was left behind – and it rankled. I suppose every virtue has its downside, even the pursuit of peace!

Joseph was a Christian – certainly not a nominal one, for his faith and beliefs permeated his whole life and were evident in his thoughts, words and actions. Early on he studied to become an accredited preacher in the Methodist Church. The circuit of Methodist churches covered a wide area and every quarter a 'Plan' was issued which indicated where each preacher would be taking the Sunday services. I remember we would scrutinise this with interest each quarter to see where my father was 'planned'. There was no public transport in our village at that time and in all weathers these journeys had to be made on his bicycle. I have now recollections of my father starting out on a Sunday morning on an eight to ten mile journey to keep his preaching appointment; indeed sometimes I accompanied him, with my mother making sure he had his sermon notes – and always a clean handkerchief!

The study involved to give this service to the church was

considerable; to cope with this with a busy household of children with no room to call a study, and after a hard day's manual work, was no mean achievement.

Family prayers were a daily feature in our home. After the evening meal, generally high tea, the Bible would be produced and my mother, using the International Bible Readings and notes, would read the set passage for the day. Then my father would pray. I can hear his quiet voice offering prayers of thankfulness for the blessings of the day and always remembering family and friends and their respective and special needs. Nobody would dream of leaving the table until these devotions were over and this routine never varied even when guests were present and whoever those guests might be.

Joseph's capacity for forgiveness and generosity and his compassion and thoughtfulness are evident in the following incident. He was a market gardener and at one stage did a retail round, travelling with his horse and van to the nearby town where he sold his produce. On one occasion his loaded cart was left overnight in the barn, when one of the village lads who was well known locally for 'getting into trouble' broke in and stole a considerable amount of the produce. The local policeman, knowing the lad's propensities and ever on the alert, managed to catch him red handed, which resulted in his having to appear at the local magistrate's court some five miles distant. Joseph, of course, was required to attend as a witness, which he did with some reluctance. Apart from the distaste he felt at having to witness against the lad who, of course, was known to him, he had to lose a precious day from his work and suffer the expense involved. In the court Joseph noticed that the lad was alone, his parents not having come to support him. There being an adjournment for lunch, Joseph, being concerned for the boy, sought him out and learning that he had no money or means of getting a meal took him out and bought him some lunch, and afterwards saw that he arrived home safely.

Joseph, with his gentle and sensitive nature, could be easily hurt by others' thoughtlessness. I remember on one occasion when, as members of his family often did, I was helping him on his retail round, a customer in one of the poorer streets became irate and made some derogatory remarks, indicating that he had been unfair

101

in his transactions with her. Joseph who was scrupulously fair in all his dealings and would under rather than overcharge his customers, was surprised and hurt by this outburst. The next week on our visit to that street I was rather surprised as we passed by her door, to hear him say, 'We'll not call there today.' The said lady then appeared at her gate calling for us to stop. Joseph, however, calmly proceeded on his way, ignoring her pleas, and never thereafter served her again! She had probably forgotten the incident and was no doubt somewhat puzzled to know why from that time she ceased to become his customer!

Although Joseph employed a lad to work with him on his smallholding, he was always kept very busy, especially at certain times of the year, and was glad of any help his family could give him. I enjoyed working with my father and even as a schoolgirl I learned to make myself useful. I loved sitting with him in the big potato clamp; it was cosy in there with its lovely earthy smell, and so companionable having him to myself and chatting together as we rubbed off the potato shoots. It was fun too tying up the lettuces. I never knew such wonderful cos lettuces as my father grew, the result perhaps of our walking up and down the rows 'hearting them up' with lengths of bass from the bundle which we had tied round our legs. Rhubarb had to be pulled and tied into bundles and then, of course, in the summer there was fruit to pick, currants, raspberries and gooseberries, and apples, pears and plums – not forgetting the sour bullace – from the trees in our garden. Yes, we were busy, but I never knew my father to become hurried, impatient or fazed, not when we may have botched a job or even sometimes deserted him when we felt we had done enough.

One task I really enjoyed was, at the end of the day, walking Daisy, our gentle and patient old carthorse, through the village to the glebe meadow which my father rented. It was always a thrill to see her, when I let her off the lead, kick up her heels and gallop round the meadow, forgetting her age and tiredness in the joy of being set free.

We also kept pigs and a few chickens. As children, when the hens would tell us when they had laid an egg – as they always did – it was good to go and feel in the nest for the lovely warm eggs we would find there. The baby chicks, too, were always a delight. The pigs we children regarded with affection and we would give them names. Two of them, whom we called Hester and Betsy, I remember as being really intelligent. They seemed to know when my father turned into the road with his horse and cart and would stand with their feet on the side of the sty and greet him noisily as he drove into the yard. But how sad we were when the time came for one of them to provide joints of pork. Besides selling the pork joints my father made parts of the pig into sausages, for which he became quite famous locally. Clarke's sausages were the best! – well, you see, the best pork went into those sausages, not just the gristle and bits which were otherwise unsaleable – oh no, Joseph's conscience and principles even impinged on his sausage making! I loved turning the handle of the sausage machine and watching the long strings of sausages emerge. Then my mother would make pork 'scratchings' which were boiled in the large copper in our kitchen.

All the family, at some stage in our lives, took turns in 'helping Dad' – and never grudgingly – my brother when home from college and my sister in time off from her nursing. I well remember spending an Easter holiday break 'setting' potatoes, walking up and down the furrows behind the plough in the field opposite our house, putting in the potatoes. I was not allowed to forget it either when I returned to my office in London with an aching back, rebelling at the unaccustomed exercise!

It was not only at work that I loved to be with my father and found his company enjoyable. He could be good company too when, with pressure of work easing occasionally, he could enjoy some light diversion from his normally busy life. He would join in ball games with us in the garden, one game coming to a disastrous climax, I remember, when he managed to divert the ball through a bedroom window. Although we were glad it was he and not we who were the culprits we were nevertheless sorry to see him incur my mother's displeasure, which put an abrupt end to our play!

Once a year a fair came to the village and I could always persuade my father to come with me to this much looked-forward-to event. Our chief delight was riding in the swing-boats – I can remember now the soft feel of the pulley ropes as we swung ourselves back and forth. The year was not complete without our swing-boat experience!

One of the worst experiences of Joseph's life came about through a rift in the life of the church. He was a steward in the little village Methodist Church and for many years worked closely and amicably with his brother-in-law, my mother's brother, who was also a close friend and a fellow lay preacher. It was a close and happy relationship and the two men had shared much together over the years. Imagine Joseph's consternation when Isaac began to question the direction in which the Methodist Church was going, its tenets and doctrines and the validity of our Minister's preaching, a Minister whom we had all held in high esteem. He contended that the church was too liberal in its views and should conform to more fundamentalistic beliefs. Besides the many discussions between the two men, the situation affected all the church members. Various meetings were called at which the Superintendent Minister was present, and at which Isaac's condemnatory views were forcibly stated. The church members were simple village folk who found the whole situation disturbing and puzzling, disturbed to find their Minister's beliefs and preaching called into question. Isaac was so vociferous in his denunciation of the church's teaching that things had to come to a head. He did much to persuade Joseph to go along with his views and, indeed, my father was very exercised in his mind and had to be sure where he stood in the matter. However, after much thought and soul-searching he knew that he could not go along with the views of his brother-in-law and friend and must give his loyalty to the church which he loved.

The outcome was that Isaac, together with a small following, including his family, left the church and eventually built and was responsible for a small mission hall situated in the village and not far from the Methodist Church where he had been a loyal member for so many years. In a small village the whole event had many unfortunate repercussions. But to my father the whole scenario was devastating. He felt betrayed and deeply hurt; indeed his whole world seemed to have fallen apart. Not only had he lost a trusted and close friend and fellow worker but, of course, family relationships were strained and it was many years before this rift was healed. To a man of peace as Joseph was, this kind of disharmony in church and family life was a great burden to bear. But through it all he showed endless patience, understanding and tolerance and I never heard an unkind or condemnatory word fall from his lips; although this could hardly be said of others involved.

Many years later Joseph's elder daughter took Isaac's wife (her aunt) into her home when she needed care in her old age and lovingly cared for her until her death, allowing all old animosities to be put in the past.

The Methodist Church building was at that time a small wooden structure with a tin roof and heated by one of the old 'tortoise' stoves. Although lovingly cared for it was not exactly a comfortable or convenient church building. The responsibility for heating the church fell to Joseph – no Sunday lie-in for him on winter mornings. He would be up betimes carrying paper and kindling wood across the field opposite our house to get the fire going ready for the ten o'clock Sunday School, and of course he saw that it was maintained throughout the day. Five services were the order of the day at that time, morning and afternoon Sunday School and morning and evening worship, with the evening service being followed by a prayer meeting. Even on the Sundays when he was taking services elsewhere on the circuit he always saw that the old 'tortoise' stove was well stoked up before he left.

Although only a small church it was very active and well-attended as, I suppose, most nonconformist village chapels were at that time. Among the various activities, at one stage a Silver Band was formed. How the instruments were obtained I know not, but Joseph, by dint of much practice, became the cornet player. My brother also was a member of the Band and I was delighted to earn sixpence for cleaning and polishing their instruments! At the Band concerts Joseph also entertained by reciting poems, one I recall being entitled 'Prayer and Potatoes'.

It was usual in those days for most children to attend a Sunday School, and so the Methodist Sunday School flourished. The various 'special occasions' were of interest to the whole village as so many of the children were involved. A much looked-forward-to event was the winter 'Treat' and concert culminating in the 'prize giving'. Tea was provided by the Sunday School staff, a tea which, by to-day's standards, the children would not, I think, consider a treat at all for, as far as I can remember, it consisted of paste sandwiches and slab cake! I suppose then it was for many considered a real 'treat'; anyway it was thoroughly enjoyed and did not take long to demolish. Then followed the concert which had entailed weeks of preparation and practices. Special singing had been rehearsed and the children had been given recitations to learn. A chairman, usually a local preacher from the circuit, was invited to announce the items, give a short talk and, of course, to present the prizes.

It was a busy time for the Sunday School staff who, having prepared the tea, now had to clear the tables and get everything ship-shape for the evening concert, as well as keep an eye on the children. On that evening the little church was packed to overflowing, as the parents were eager to come and hear their children perform. A great air of excitement prevailed which as a child I remember grew to great heights on one occasion as we spied our village schoolmaster in the audience!

Then, to crown all our excitement and anticipation, came the Prize-giving. Prizes were given for attendance, a register having been kept throughout the year. The number of attendances made was reflected in the quality of the prize and there was always much speculation among us as to where we had come in the scheme of things.

As an avid reader, and books not being easily obtainable in those days, how I looked forward to receiving my prize from the chairman, inscribed with my name and number of attendances made. I always hoped it would be a *large* book and so provide lots of reading matter!

Joseph, of course, had his part to play in this yearly event, for the old tortoise stove had to be lit early and heat ensured throughout the day. Afterwards, of course, there was the task of clearing up in order to make the church ship-shape and in order for the next Sunday services – not that he ever complained or begrudged the time and work involved.

The other main Sunday School event was the Summer Outing. In my early childhood this outing was always to Hockley Woods, some nine or ten miles distant, although later, with mechanised transport, we ventured farther afield. The journey to Hockley Woods was undertaken by Joseph with his horse and cart. The wooden chapel seats were placed in the cart and it was surprising how many children could be accommodated. It says much for the patience and placidity of Joseph's horse that it was not fazed in carrying the crowd of noisy happy children, but calmly and steadily covered the miles until we reached our destination. The grown-ups followed in whatever forms of transport were available, bicycles coming to the fore!

Journeys outside the village at that time were rare and this was a long anticipated event; everybody was happy and excited and, looking back, it always seemed the day was warm and sunny. We took packed lunches and picnicked in the woods, although there was a stall where we could buy drinks and sweets. The main, or only, source of amusement, as I remember, were the swings and see-saws. I always envied and looked with awe at the 'big' children who were daring enough, with the aid of a 'pusher', to send the swings flying higher than we younger ones dared to go. On the way home there was always a sing-song as we jogged along the country roads, the Sunday School songs being the favourites. The villagers who had stayed at home would come out to welcome us back and how excitedly the children would recount the events of the day before going happily to bed, where they no doubt lived it all over again in their dreams.

What simple unalloyed pleasure those long ago Sunday School outings provided!

Joseph had a dream. He dreamed and longed for a beautiful new church building. My dictionary gives the definition of a dream as 'A distant hope or ideal – probably unobtainable'. The first part of that definition certainly applied to Joseph's dream but he refused, against all odds, to believe it was unobtainable. To all intents and purposes it seemed so, for to be realised, where was such a sizeable sum of money to come from? None of the church members, however generous, could provide any substantial amount, and there were no benefactors in sight! However a church meeting was called and the result was the inauguration of a Building Fund. It was certainly a slow growing 'acorn' from which the 'oak tree' was to grow.

Everybody was keen to do their bit, although some were very dubious about their goal ever being reached.

Various fund-raising events followed and continued for many years – it was no short term project. Many hours of thought and labour went into arranging bazaars, garden parties and social evenings. The children did their part (and, incidentally many had grown into adulthood before they saw the results of their efforts!). Each child had a Building Fund book and recruited subscribers from their friends and relatives, in the main the subscriptions being just a few coppers or less weekly. It should be remembered that all this work and giving was confined to a small circle of people belonging to a small church and a small village.

As a child I remember how we all participated in the Building Fund scheme. Then in my teens when I was commuting to London I persuaded an acquaintance of mine who was in the confectionery business to sell me chocolate on a wholesale basis, which I then sold to my office colleagues at a small profit – more fodder for the Building Fund! Right from the start a quarterly social was held to which everybody brought their contributions and what happy exciting occasions these always were as we watched our 'Fund' slowly but surely growing. I have recollections of my father sitting at a table in the church counting the money as it was brought in and our excitement and joy as the total was announced.

Joseph was adamant, and the church members agreed, that when the new church was eventually built it must be free of debt. Debt in any form was abhorrent to him and he felt that what applied in his private life was no less important for the church, so no mortgages or borrowed money were an option as far as he was concerned.

And so it was that after many years of unflagging effort and optimism, Joseph's dream at last came true. Plans were passed and the building actually began to take shape on the piece of land adjoining the little wooden chapel, which, incidentally, had many years previously been moved from the next village. Then the day of the stone-laying ceremony arrived, a truly exciting event but, even so, not to be compared with the wonderful day when our new church was actually opened for worship, the result of all our effort and the culmination of our dreams!

When completed it was indeed a beautiful little church. A small pipe organ was donated by a church which had no further use for it, as were the wooden pews. The Sunday School appropriately presented the font from which future children would be baptised. Various items were donated in memory of former members, some of whom had played an active part when the Building Fund had first been mooted. Years later when Joseph himself had passed on, a cross was erected over the pulpit in his memory.

The opening ceremony was indeed a memorable occasion in which the whole village participated, and not only the village, for most of the churches in the Methodist circuit were represented. Most of the local preachers who had served us over the years in our little tin-roofed building were there, and also notable figures in the wider Methodist connection came to rejoice with us on this auspicious occasion.

The new church was packed to overflowing; the vestries also being full some of the congregation had perforce to remain outside! The atmosphere was electric, the speakers inspired and joy and happiness prevailed.

Although Joseph's aim had been to have the church opened free

Interior of new church, with chairs up the aisle on the opening day.

of debt, owing to some unforeseen expenses there was found, in the end, to be a shortfall. The presiding Minister, hearing of this situation, made the appeal for the dream of a debt-free church to be realised – and it was. The money poured in from generous donations until there was actually an excess of the amount required.

It has been said that 'Methodism was born in song', and certainly no Methodist gathering is complete without the singing of some of the grand old Charles Wesley hymns. This occasion was no exception, and I think they were never sung with more fervour, the theme of joy and thankfulness running throughout.

Joseph's dream had at last come true and there were tears of joy in his eyes at the end of that wonderful day. To crown my parents' happiness my brother, who by that time had entered the Methodist Ministry, on the following Sunday preached the first sermon in our lovely new church. It was fortuitous that the building was finished in 1938, the year before the outbreak of war, during which it would have been doubtful if building work could have gone ahead. The following year my own wedding was the first to be solemnised there. My father served as Steward in the church until his death some years later.

Sadly, the church of Joseph's dream is no longer in existence. Young people having drifted away from the village and the ageing congregation dwindling, after some fifty years it was deemed unviable for the church to carry on its ministry. How sad that its life should have been so comparatively short. I am profoundly glad that my parents never lived to see the day of its closure.

Perhaps, after all, those who may have thought Joseph an unremarkable man could have been wrong!